Know Yourself, Know Your Money

I praise you because I am fearfully and wonderfully made; your works are wonderful, I know that full well.

PSALM 139:14

Know Yourself, Know Your Money

Discover WHY you
handle money the
way you do, and
WHAT to do about it!

RACHEL CRUZE

RAMSEY
PRESS

Published by Ramsey Press, The Lampo Group, LLC
Franklin, Tennessee 37064

Library of Congress Cataloging-in-Publication Data

Names: Cruze, Rachel, author.
Title: Know yourself, know your money : discover why you handle money the way you do, and what to do about it! / Rachel Cruze.
Description: Franklin : Ramsey Press, 2021.
Identifiers: LCCN 2020032403 (print) | LCCN 2020032404 (ebook) | ISBN 9781942121312 (hardcover) | ISBN 9781942121336 | ISBN 9781942121329 (ebook)
Subjects: LCSH: Finance, Personal.
Classification: LCC HG179 .C788 2021 (print) | LCC HG179 (ebook) | DDC 332.024--dc23
LC record available at https://lccn.loc.gov/2020032403
LC ebook record available at https://lccn.loc.gov/2020032404

ISBN: 978-1-9421-2131-2

Editors: Jennifer Day, Rachel Knapp
Cover Design: Chris Carrico
Interior Design: Mandi Cofer

Printed in the United States of America
21 22 23 24 25 WRZ 5 4 3 2 1

To Winston.

I love that you are the person in this world who knows me the best. I feel known by you and loved by you. Your approach to growing yourself is one that has not only strengthened our marriage but my pursuit to grow and know myself even more. Thank you for always being there, and for encouraging and fighting for me in this life. I love you so much.

CONTENTS

PART 1
Discovering Your Personal Money Mindset

PART 2
Discovering What You *Do* with Money and Why

ACKNOWLEDGMENTS

This book would not be the same if it weren't for the many people who helped shape what it is. I am forever grateful to work with an incredible team who is so passionate about helping people discover more about themselves so they can win in money and life! A special word of thanks to:

Winston Cruze, for your support during this two-year project while you had a major project going on yourself, I was pregnant, and we were building a house.

Dave Ramsey, for teaching me so much and pushing me to get the best book out of me that you knew was there.

Jennifer Day, I have said it before and I will say it again: you are an angel sent from heaven. Thank you for all your work and making this book what it is!

Ami McConnell, thank you for shaping my words and stories into a process that people will actually want to read! You were incredibly helpful to this project.

Preston Cannon, for leading this project from start to finish and adding humor along the way.

Katie Crenshaw, for your leadership and encouragement. I'm glad you're my boss.

Amy McCollom, for coordinating all the millions of details to make sure we actually had a book!

Rachel Knapp, for your copyediting skills. You are always a pleasure to work with and so good at what you do.

Chris Carrico and Brad Dennison, Brad Imburgia, Will Smith, and Seth Farmer for the design element and how your gifts make this book look incredible.

Heidi Egloff, Cory Mabry, and Caitlin Cofield, for the best publicity and marketing minds on the planet. So thankful for you all.

Jeremy Breland, Suzanne Simms, Jen Sieversten, Andy Barton, Julia Mynhier, Erin Drury, Naomi Parton, Russ Sellars, Cathy Shanks, Alena Drehmann, Tim Smith, Natalie Wilson, Shane Emerson, and too many others to mention for their time, leadership, prayers, and hard work throughout this process.

FOREWORD BY DAVE RAMSEY

When you grow up in a noble, hillbilly household like I did, stories and sayings become part of who you are. Partly because you
hear them over and over again. And partly because they carry so
much truth. I remember many times when I was a little kid, my
dad would say, "Ninety percent of solving a problem is realizing
there is one." That's true whether the problem is with the trans-
mission in your car or the problem is with you.

When I went broke many years ago, I made the mistake most
financial people make. I thought the way to fix my personal
finance problems was to come up with a different mathematical
strategy. All I needed was some brilliant breakthrough with the
numbers. Then, the huge hole of debt I'd dug for myself and my
family would magically disappear.

But the math was not the problem. The real breakthrough
was discovering that the guy in my mirror was the problem. Oh,
and by the way—he was also the solution. I couldn't change the
numbers. I was millions of dollars in debt no matter which way I

looked at it. I couldn't change that, but I *could* change me. I could stop doing stupid stuff with money. I could learn about God's ways of handling money—and do that instead.

Today, thirty years after that moment of self-discovery, my team and I have now taught millions and millions of people that personal finance is not about the math. Handling your money—*winning* with money—is all about behavior. We have a saying for that too: personal finance is 80 percent behavior and 20 percent head knowledge. Knowing what to do with your money is the easy part. Actually *doing* it is the hard part.

Changing your behavior is tough work. You have to first understand your own personal strengths and weaknesses. Why do you make the choices you do with money? That's not an easy—or comfortable—question to answer sometimes. But by discovering what your strengths and weaknesses are, you can learn how to offset those weaknesses and accentuate your strengths. And that? That's fuel on the fire of behavior change. It will lead to huge breakthroughs with your money, your relationships, and your life.

My daughter Rachel Cruze grew up living the money principles I started teaching when she was a baby. The poor kid had no idea how weird her family was! If I'm the expert on how to use those principles to clean up a money mess and build wealth, then Rachel is the expert on how to live them out from the very beginning. Every day, she talks with people who are struggling with money—from stage, through *The Rachel Cruze Show*, and in her bestselling books. Her message is clear: you can live a life you love.

But she's been listening too. As people shared their stories, Rachel dug into the *why* behind the choices they made—so she could help them make better ones. And that's what this book is all about.

Through a series of different lenses, Rachel will walk you through your own path of self-discovery. You'll learn how the way you grew up influences your money decisions. You'll start to understand your real money fears and how to face them. You'll get to the bottom of what motivates you to spend and save money. And most importantly, Rachel will help you use all you've learned to transform your money and your life. By the time you finish turning these pages, you'll be equipped to change your behaviors and finally make real progress in one of life's most stressful subjects: money. Your relationships will be touched. Your future will be changed. And certainly, your bank account will be affected.

You won't be able to stop reading, so set aside plenty of time for this one, folks. Get ready to learn about yourself—and then get ready to get to work!

INTRODUCTION

When I was growing up, my parents used to read to us every night. The memory of this still makes me smile. I'd crawl into the bed with my older sister, Denise, and my younger brother, Daniel, and Mom's sweet, soothing voice would help us drift off to sleep, sometimes before the story ended. And when Dad read to us? That was the best! Nobody was falling asleep for that! He would always use crazy voices for the characters or change their names to funnier ones. My all time favorite was when he was reading a Bible story and replaced the word *disciples* with *goobers*. We laughed *so* hard. We thought he was the funniest dad on the planet.

One particular bedtime story stands out in my mind. The book was called *The Treasure Tree* by John Trent and Gary Smalley. In this book, there are four animals—a lion, a beaver, an otter, and a golden retriever. Together they set out on an adventure, looking for four golden keys that would lead them to the treasure tree. The animals have a map to help guide them, but they have another advantage too: the unique way each of them views the world.

That unique view is actually what helps each of them overcome obstacles along the way. By the end of the book, the lion's leadership, the beaver's organization, the otter's quick wit, and the golden retriever's loyalty help get them to the treasure tree.

Now that I look back on it as an adult, I realize this was a pretty deep book. As a kid, it held our attention because the story was entertaining and the illustrations were beautiful. But there was more to it than that. Since it was a longer book, my parents would read just one chapter every night. And as we listened to them read each night, we could easily see who in our family was most like each of the animals. We knew for sure my dad was the lion, my mom was the golden retriever, Denise was the beaver, Daniel was a good mix of the lion and otter, and I was the otter.

I remember, even as a ten-year-old, relating so much to that otter. She was spunky, fun, and always had a bright outlook on life. As we read, I loved it when my family would point to the otter and say, "Rachel, that's exactly what you would do!" In fact, as each one of our personalities showed up in the book, we would celebrate. This gave me confidence in who I was. I felt known and understood, a part of something special. *The Treasure Tree* helped me begin to see *me*.

This memory is special to me for a couple of reasons. I love that we spent time together as a family, even if it was just reading together at night. I also love that identifying with the otter helped me understand myself more clearly. I began to notice that I related in a unique way to my family and to the world. I learned each person in my family had strengths to lean into and weaknesses to overcome. It even gave me new language to communicate better with others. Understanding myself and the people around me was both fascinating and helpful. I was hooked!

Whether we learn about ourselves through life experience or counseling, through books on topics like birth order, or through personality assessments like the DiSC profile, Myers-Briggs, or the Enneagram—self-awareness is *powerful*. We're all complex people with different stories and ways of viewing the world, but understanding who we are and how we're wired—our past, our strengths and weaknesses, our fears and dreams—helps us know why we make the choices we do. And once we know the *why* behind our decisions and habits, we can choose to make different ones, better ones.

At Ramsey Solutions, we've helped millions of people find financial peace. Since my dad started the company over twenty-five years ago, we've been teaching the intimidating topic of personal finance in a way that anyone in any walk of life can understand and apply it. It's our passion. Want to know how to win with money? We can help! Budgeting, getting out of debt, investing, wealth building, giving generously, teaching kids about money, paying for college without student loans—we've got all of that and more. And you can count on the fact that I'll talk about some of those money principles in this book too! But while those principles are critical for winning with money, they're about *how* to handle your money, not *why* you handle money the way you do. And there's a big difference between the two.

My friend Amanda has always *loved* to shop. Finding good deals is a sport to her. And while she's in a good place with it now, it used to be so stressful for her and her husband. No matter how much money they made, Amanda almost always spent more than they had. Her husband tried to be understanding and patient, but he was deeply frustrated. In her late thirties, knowing her marriage was on rocky ground, Amanda decided to go to counseling to figure out the root of her problem.

You know what she discovered? Her shopping habit was actually a reaction to growing up with excessively frugal parents who rarely spent money. Her parents were precious people who had learned to survive with very little. But they would do things like save the bags out of cereal boxes "just in case." After eighteen years of living like this, once she was on her own, Amanda started shopping just because she could. Realizing this about herself in counseling was a lightbulb moment, and it was the beginning of permanently shifting her buying habits from that point forward. She still enjoys shopping today, but she's no longer driven by the impulse to do it—and it's no longer a source of conflict in her marriage. She figured out the *why* behind her behavior and it changed everything.

Amanda isn't alone. I was talking with psychologist and best-selling author Dr. Henry Cloud, and he put it this way, "How you're glued together has everything to do with how you spend your money." There's a reason you make the decisions you do with money. And if you can understand why you handle money the way you do, you can decide to make better choices and, ultimately, achieve a whole new level of financial peace. When you know yourself, you'll be able to better answer questions like:

- What do I believe about money and why?
- Why do I keep making the same money mistakes?
- Why can't my spouse and I get on the same page about money?
- What do I need to change about myself so that I can change my family tree?

The more you understand yourself, the better you'll be at talking about and handling your money. Do you know what that means? It means you can get out of debt faster—and permanently. You can partner with your spouse more effectively. You can build wealth and reach your goals more quickly. *You can actually create and live a life you love!*

Know Yourself, Know Your Money is all about self-discovery—learning what you believe about money and understanding why you do and don't do certain things with it. In part 1, we'll look at discovering your personal money mindset: what you learned about money during childhood, how you're uniquely wired to spend money, what fears you have about money, and why you respond to money mistakes the way you do. Then in part 2, we'll look at what motivates your money behaviors: why you choose to spend, save, and give like you do and how committed you are to winning with money for the long haul. As you read these sections, my hope is you'll learn a lot about yourself as well as the people closest to you.

But make no mistake: I didn't write this book so you would have some self-awareness and "aha" moments and then move on to the next thing. I wrote this book so you'd take this new knowledge and put it into action. So in the conclusion, we'll review what you've learned about yourself, and then I'll show you how to put those insights into action so you can make real progress with your money and in your life. Because, as it turns out, when you improve your money, you also improve your relationships and your future.

When you understand why you handle money the way you do, you can build on your strengths and change your bad habits for good—so that you can do the things that matter most to you. This is going to be a *game changer.* So let's get started!

PART 1

Discovering Your Personal Money Mindset

CHAPTER 1

Your Childhood Money Classroom

Spaghetti night changed my life. I was in second grade, and I was having dinner at my best friend's house. Katie Thompson lived down the street from me, and we had been friends since before I could remember. I had been to her house dozens of times to play, and she'd been to mine a lot. Our moms were good friends too. As a mom myself now, I know that when my kids play well with my friend's kids, it's the absolute best. It must have been a total win for our moms that Katie and I were attached at the hip.

That night at dinner, though, something happened. And when I look back, it was a pretty profound moment in my life. It was getting to be dinner time, and Katie's mom told us we were going to have spaghetti. I was thrilled. My mom made spaghetti all the time at our house, and it was one of my favorites. (Even to this day, it's one of my go-to dinners!) But when we sat down to actually eat, something wasn't right.

The noodles were way longer than they were supposed to be. My mom always broke ours in half. These noodles were so long they seemed to never end. The sauce was dark red, almost brown, and worse, there were these disgusting-looking balls of meat sitting in the middle of the dish (aka meatballs—which I'd never seen before). Spaghetti sauce was *supposed* to be bright red with tiny pieces of ground-up meat in it. And where was the bread? There was supposed to be bread! What were we supposed to dip into the extra sauce on our plate?

As I sat there in confusion, Katie's family happily dug in to the meal using their spoons to twirl the spaghetti around their forks to eat. At home we cut our spaghetti with a fork, and every now and again, you'd hear a slurp from someone at the table. Katie's mom poured us milk to drink, which was so strange to me. In our (very southern) house, the only thing you drank at dinner was sweet tea. What I was experiencing at Katie's was all wrong in my mind. *No, no, no!* This was *not* spaghetti, and this was *not* how spaghetti night was supposed to go! My little world was shattered.

It's one of the first memories I have of realizing not everyone did things the way I did. Until that moment, I just assumed spaghetti only looked one way—and I'm pretty sure Katie thought the same thing! She expected a long-noodle, dark-sauce, meatball dinner with milk, and I expected a short-noodle, bright-red-sauce, bread dinner with sweet tea. We can all have the same formula for something as simple as spaghetti: A spaghetti dinner equals noodles, meat, and sauce. But there are a million ways to make it, and as a result, it can look and taste very different from one house to another.

I find the same is true for money. Each home is unique. Every parent is different. How you grew up and the environment you were raised in shaped your money beliefs and your habits with money in very specific ways. That's why the first step in understanding why we handle money the way we do is to begin with our childhood. Because as children grow, more is caught than taught, meaning children absorb a lot about money without even realizing it. For some, money is stressful and secretive. For others, it's peaceful and positive. It's all the same basic ingredients—money, income, bills, goals—but it can look and feel very different from one house to another.

HOW MY MONEY STORY BEGAN

How and why we relate to money the way we do as adults is largely influenced by our parents or the people who took care of us growing up. This is true no matter what kind of home we grew up in, regardless of whether we grew up with one parent, two parents, or relatives.

My money story began during the hardest financial season my parents would ever face. I was born in April, and they filed bankruptcy papers in September of the same year. My older sister was about three years old, so with a brand-new baby, a toddler, and—as Dad says all the time—"a marriage hanging on by a thread," they hit rock bottom. *Hard.* It took a good five years for them to climb out of that hole—right around the same time as my earliest memories.

I don't remember the initial crash of the bankruptcy. What I remember is the aftermath and what became a new way of living with money for our family. My parents started talking about money with each other, they budgeted what little money they did have, and they avoided debt like it was the plague. We shopped at consignment stores for clothes, never took a vacation, and only ever saw the inside of a restaurant on our birthdays. That was how I thought everyone lived. My parents' perspective on debt, budgeting, and saving deeply impacted my own perspective.

Because of my parents' hard work after that soul-crushing bankruptcy, I was able to learn firsthand the value of managing money well. I learned my income is my biggest wealth-building tool—so I never took on any debt and I never will. In fact, I've been working Dave Ramsey's Baby Steps my entire life! I don't say that to pat myself on the back, but to show you how big of an impact parents have on our money outlook.

Your story may not involve something as drastic as bankruptcy, but the way your parents viewed and handled money during your childhood is extremely important for you to understand. Your childhood household was your money classroom. As an adult, you may handle money much like your parents did when you were a child, or you may have deliberately chosen to modify—or do the exact opposite of—what your parents did. Regardless, we each learned lessons there that we've taken into adulthood. Some are good habits and healthy views on money that help us. And some are lessons we wish we could *unlearn*.

POPCORN

Growing up, one of the biggest treats for us Ramsey kids was going to the movie theater. Part of the fun of going to the movies was the full experience—the movie, the Coke, *and* the popcorn. One year, my mom bought an extra-large bag of popcorn there so we could have free refills. At the end of every movie, Mom would dump out any uneaten popcorn, fold the bag neatly, and stuff it into her purse. The next time we went to the theater, she would take out that same bag, unfold it, and get her free "refill." Sometimes she would even send one of us kids to get it!

One time, I was the lucky refiller. A kid working the concession stand just looked at me and that oily, creased, obviously used popcorn bag. Clearly confused, he asked, "Has this bag been used before?" I felt like I had been caught for insider trading! I just gave him a nervous grin, took my refill, and walked quickly back into the theater.

That's right, ladies and gentlemen, we'd technically been stealing popcorn from that place for years! We told that story one night at dinner a few years ago, and my dad was dying: "Sharon! I cannot believe you stole popcorn from the movie theater!"

"David," she said in her sweet southern accent. "I wasn't stealing. I was being economical."

Now, I can tell you that today I have a deep conviction to buy popcorn anywhere popcorn is sold to make up for all those years of "free" refills. That level of "economy" is not a habit I took with me into adulthood!

Of course, this is a lighthearted example of how our childhoods impact us as adults, but these experiences aren't always lighthearted. Whether it's frugal living or lavish spending or somewhere in the middle, we need to spend some time exploring our money classroom to discover how it's shaped us.

DIFFERENT PERSPECTIVES

As you think about how you were raised, keep in mind that you and your siblings may have different perspectives of what it was like growing up in your house. We're all wired differently. Our passions, our fears, and our dreams are different. Even if you had siblings who grew up in the same house, and even if you had similar external experiences, the way you guys all *perceived* and *internalized* those experiences can be very different. The same goes for your best friend. The same goes for your spouse, if you're married. The same goes for your brother-in-law.

Here's an example: My parents were right in the middle when it came to strictness in their parenting. If I was at a sleepover and a friend's parent wanted me to call home for permission to watch a certain movie, my parents would always say yes. I mean, it's not like we wanted to watch *Silence of the Lambs* in the fifth grade. So they were definitely not strict about movies.

They were, however, *very* strict on curfew. My older sister, Denise, had it the hardest. Poor firstborn. As the middle child, I had a little more wiggle room. And when it came to my younger brother, Daniel, he basically got away with anything. As a mom with two older daughters and a younger son, I totally understand that now.

Denise was a junior in high school when I was a freshman. I was *thrilled* when she got her driver's license. It gave me a real taste of freedom. We could do things without my parents having to drive us! Every Wednesday night, Denise and I would go to our church's youth group. Afterward, we'd all go out to the same Mexican restaurant down the street from the church, just a bunch of teenagers devouring chips, queso, and water. We were so cheap we wouldn't even buy a Coke! But thanks to Mom and Dad's example, we did always leave a tip.

One Wednesday night as we were headed out the door for youth group, Dad yelled, "Be back tonight!" We looked at each other, puzzled. *What did* that *mean?* It wasn't a complete thought, but we were already running late, so we didn't stop to ask questions. As we were buckling our seat belts, Denise said, "We have to be back by nine thirty." I disagreed. I said that since he didn't give us a specific time, ten was fine. She responded that Dad always said she needed to be in by nine thirty, and if she was a minute late, she'd be grounded. For some reason, Mom and Dad let me stay out until ten sometimes, so I used my natural sales ability and convinced Denise to stay out later.

When we got home at ten, Mom and Dad asked why we were late. Denise glared at me. Sure enough, she was right. I was truly shocked. Dad reminded us he had never let us stay out past nine thirty on a school night. And that even if he hadn't given us a specific time, the expectation had already been set. Thankfully, there was no grounding for either of us, but I'm still convinced, decades later, I was in the right.

See? Two different kids, two different personalities, two different experiences—same set of parents. As we unpack the dynamics of your childhood home, remember that your siblings may have different views of how your parents handled money. Heck, even your parents probably have different perspectives and memories when it comes to how they raised you. That's okay. What matters is understanding how it affected *you*.

HOW WE LEARN ABOUT MONEY GROWING UP

When we look at our childhood money classrooms, there are really two ways we learned about money: what our parents communicated *emotionally* and what they communicated *verbally*. We experience emotional communication through the positive or negative vibes we get about something even if we can't pinpoint exactly why. When emotional communication is positive, we feel calm, and when it's negative, we feel stressed. This type of communication is as power-ful—if not more powerful—than verbal communication.

Growing up, you may have sensed that money was stressful. Maybe you can't say why specifically, but you had a general uneas-iness talking about anything money-related. Maybe you could feel the tension in the room when your dad found out about some-thing your mom bought. Sometimes the anxiety was so thick you felt like you could cut it with a knife. Or maybe you had a hard time telling your parents you needed money for school because you suspected they would react negatively. You felt like you were walking around on eggshells without knowing why.

On the other end of the emotional spectrum, you may have sensed a calm and secure feeling about money. If the car broke down, it didn't faze your parents. They just took it to the repair shop and got it fixed. If your winter coat tore accidentally, it wasn't a big deal. You just got another one. You didn't hesitate about asking for something you needed. You didn't always get what you wanted, but buying things wasn't stressful. There was a sense of stability and control.

We also learned about money through verbal communi-cation—what was (or wasn't) said in our homes. Some house-holds were verbally closed. Your parents didn't talk about money in front of you. Maybe they didn't talk about it at all. There was never any discussion around the dinner table about debt, budget-ing, or investing. Plus, you knew *not* to talk about some things, like money, religion, politics, sex—or all of the above—and so you never did. There was no discussion, no conflict, no give-and-take—just an absence of communication.

For other households, money was an open and ongoing con-versation. Maybe your parents talked about budgeting. Maybe they discussed putting off one purchase to make room for a different one. Maybe the family voted on how to spend money in a particular category of the budget. This dialogue may have been peaceful: You heard calm and controlled conversations about money. Or on the flip side, you may have heard constant fighting and yelling. Arguing is still open communication because even though there's conflict, you are talking about the issues.

These two types of communication—emotional and verbal—intersect with one another to create four quadrants:

These quadrants represent the four major money classrooms.

Quadrant 1: The Anxious Classroom
Quadrant 2: The Unstable Classroom
Quadrant 3: The Unaware Classroom
Quadrant 4: The Secure Classroom

As we explore each quadrant, you might find yours quickly. That's great! But don't skip over the other quadrants. Read about each of them so you can learn how other people in your life grew up. It will help you understand why your spouse handles money the way he does or why your best friend sees money a certain way. You might gain insight into the dynamic your parents have or why the guy you're dating spends money so freely. Doing so will likely build the empathy you have for the people you love—and lead to better relationships.

As you explore the quadrants in chapters 2 and 3 and reflect on your childhood, ask yourself these questions:

- What did I hear about money growing up?
- What did I see when it came to money?
- What did I experience or feel from my parent or parents regarding money?

This includes your entire childhood from birth until you moved out on your own. Look for the defining moments that shaped you and how you view money. These are formative memories, like my spaghetti dinner night, that taught you something significant about money. I call them *Milestone Moments*. They will help you connect the dots from your childhood and to your money behaviors as an adult.

Also, if you split time between your mom's house and your dad's house growing up or a parent got married at some point, there's a good chance you experienced more than one quadrant growing up. Keep that in mind as you continue to read.

CHAPTER 2

Stressed Money Classrooms

The first two money classrooms we'll look at are the emotionally stressed quadrants: Anxious (emotionally stressed and verbally closed) and Unstable (emotionally stressed and verbally open). We'll look at the emotionally calm quadrants in chapter 3.

QUADRANT 1: ANXIOUS CLASSROOM
Emotionally Stressed and Verbally Closed

You grew up in an Anxious Classroom if you felt anxiety or tension around money, and money was never or rarely talked about. One of my friends shared with me how he learned money was not a pleasant or easy topic for his parents. As a young boy, he went to the grocery store with his mom every week. And every week she would buy day-old, expired bread. He never thought about it until he went to the store with a friend and his mom. He watched as his friend's mom pulled out and examined several loaves before deciding on one. Curious, he asked what she was doing. She explained that she was looking at the expiration date to find the freshest bread stocked for the day.

The next time my friend went to the store with his own mom, he suggested she look for the freshest bread. His mom refused. She said, "Expired bread is half the price, and we'll eat it quickly anyway. Every cent we save helps make sure we can pay all of our bills at the end of the month."

His mom didn't say much, but her words hit him like a ton of bricks. At his age he wasn't even sure what "bills" were, but he easily read the expression on his mom's face when she got to the checkout line. She looked anxiously over every purchase, waiting and holding her breath for the cashier to announce the total amount due. She would then carefully count out the exact amount for the clerk, down to the last penny. Sometimes she would even hold a few items back and choose not to purchase them in the end because she didn't have enough money. This was a Milestone Moment for my friend. He learned money was extremely stressful and that every single penny mattered.

If you grew up in the Anxious Classroom, you probably observed your parents' money habits rather than hearing them discussed. You probably felt the tension rather than hearing an argument. Growing up, you might not have felt the freedom to ask questions. The tough reality of living in this quadrant is not just the lack of information; it's also the heightened emotional state in the home—either in general or specifically around the topic of money.

Challenges for Quadrant 1: Anxious Classroom

No matter which quadrant you grew up in, there will be challenges to overcome. Let's look at the biggest challenges for growing up in the Anxious Classroom.

Money Talks. You may find it challenging to open up and talk about the shape of your finances or the feelings you have about money. Does your spouse (or anyone) know how stressed you are about making ends meet? Have you shared with anyone that you're scared and you don't know if you're doing enough for retirement? Learning how to navigate healthy money conversations may be difficult initially, but I would challenge you to start talking about money even when it's hard. There are no perfect people, and you won't always get it right—but that's okay! Press in and talk about your money with the people you trust the most.

You could start by letting your spouse or a family member know that you have a hard time talking about money. Sometimes just saying that out loud can turn into a good conversation. But take it a step further and talk about *why* it's hard for you. Then share your desire to talk about money more freely and openly. You could even ask your spouse if they have suggestions for how to improve the communication around money. It's not going to feel natural at first, but the more you talk about your money, the easier it's going to get. If you're single, find a family member or good friend and do the same thing. A good friend who knows you well will help you look at your situation honestly and will have new insights about how to achieve your goals. Your life, your marriage, and even your kids will have such an advantage if these conversations are open and honest.

Fear. Fear is a powerful emotion. It can stop you from doing the most important things. Have you ever noticed that when you don't talk about a problem your fear actually grows larger? The problem starts to feel bigger and scarier and worse than it really is. We'll spend a whole chapter on fear later in the book. But for any of you who grew up in the Anxious Classroom, you'll need to face any fears you have about the lack of money. Identifying your specific fears and creating a tactical, detailed monthly plan for your money will help you do this because it removes the unknown. This plan is your budget. Think about it as your road map. Be intentional and write out exactly where you want your money to go—and be detailed! Once you set your budget, it will tell you what you can and can't do with every dollar—and give you the direction you need to move forward with confidence.

Grace. As you think about what your household was like growing up, it's important to have grace for your parents or whoever raised you. This is true no matter which quadrant you grew up in because not a single person is perfect. Money is a hard topic for most people. Some parents didn't have the emotional capacity to talk about money because of the stress they were under. Other parents didn't know how to do it well. Most parents really did the best they could with what they knew at the time. My goal for you isn't to make excuses for your parents, but to simply realize and own the truth. Holding a grudge against anyone for past money mistakes will only hurt you. It's important for you to work through frustrations and hurt, but the end goal is to forgive them.

If you're having trouble extending grace, I would challenge you to really reflect on your parents' childhoods. When I talk to people who grew up in the Anxious Classroom, I find that if their parents didn't openly talk about money, most likely their grandparents didn't communicate about money either (or a number of other life topics for that matter). How did your parents grow up? Was money crazy tight? Were they allowed to talk about taboo topics like money? What beliefs did they have about money? Maybe they didn't have the tools they needed to handle money wisely. Maybe they were so hurt from their own childhood that they reacted by going to the opposite extreme. Maybe they thought they were protecting you. Whatever it was, remember: We're not here to talk badly about your parents or gloss over their mistakes with excuses, but to tell the truth and show them grace.

QUADRANT 2: UNSTABLE CLASSROOM
Emotionally Stressed and Verbally Open

People who grew up in the Unstable Classroom usually recognize it immediately because it was *seen* and *heard*. In these households, money was a source of conflict. Parents argued about it between themselves, with the kids, with extended family, sometimes even with strangers. The arguments may have been public or private, but the emotions in the house were charged—potentially even explosive.

Maybe your parents fought about how money should be handled during a particular season of life. Or maybe anxiety and pressure were the norm. It's common for those in this quadrant to hear the same fight over and over. If these money issues were never resolved, or they couldn't come to an agreement, the tension may have continued to build and caused the couple to call it quits. Sadly, fights about money are one of the leading causes of divorce in America today.[1] You might know the truth of that all too well—whether in your parents' marriage or even your own.

In the Unstable Classroom, you frequently experience very negative emotions. You often feel fearful, anxious, and unloved because you hear no a lot from your parents (usually in a short-tempered way). But it's not limited to negative emotions. Growing up could have felt like an emotional roller coaster because the emotions would swing unexpectedly between the negative and positive. This could often lead to feelings of instability and even chaos.

One friend who grew up in this classroom remembers she never knew how her parents would respond when she asked for something. She heard no a lot, and her parents' quick and sometimes harsh negative responses created emotional confusion. There was such frequent, high stress around money that any kind of ask—from a request for a certain kind of cereal at the grocery store to going to the movies with her friends—could be met with either a calm "sure" or an angry "NO!" She never knew what to expect!

At the store, her mom would say they couldn't afford brand-name toothpaste, and then a few days later, her dad would say, "Let's all go shopping! We got our tax return check!" And off they would go to the mall for a huge shopping spree or to buy three carts full of food at the grocery store, including the cereal she'd just been denied. There was no consistency or way to anticipate the response. She said it felt like whiplash. Those were Milestone Moments for her. Now, as an adult, she looks back and knows her parents struggled to pay the bills each month because they didn't have a plan or live intentionally with their money (her words, not mine).

I was talking to my parents recently about my childhood money classroom. I feel like I grew up in a Secure Classroom. It wasn't perfect, but it was healthy. It was really interesting because when I told my parents that, they just looked at each other and smiled. When I asked why they reacted that way, Dad said, "You only have memories about five years *after* the bankruptcy. It was definitely an Unstable Classroom for many years—you just don't remember."

We all had a good laugh because the Ramseys are self-proclaimed hillbillies. We would for sure fall on the "open" side of the verbal communication scale—and we know how to fight. When we're all together at least three good debates are going on about things as serious as theology and as minor as what temperature best smokes a pork butt to perfection. (Google has been our saving grace for years—we've ended many debates with a quick search for the right answer!)

I can only imagine what those unstable years were like for my parents. What's surprising is that I asked my sister if she had any Unstable Classroom memories from our childhood, and she didn't either. That's really good news for all of us as parents. It really *is* possible to learn, grow, and change, making a new start for your family!

It's worth mentioning that one benefit of growing up in an Unstable Classroom is that your parents were at least willing to communicate about money, even if their communication wasn't in the healthiest way. When we talk about things openly, even if it's in a charged way, change is possible. Open disagreements signal a willingness to communicate. This is really an amazing gift because you can't fix a problem you don't know about.

Challenges for Quadrant 2: Unstable Classroom

Expectations of Conflict. For those who've grown up in this quadrant, one of the challenges you may face is anticipating that talking about money will always be emotionally charged. You may find yourself waiting for the other shoe to drop and even expect painful conflict. If you're single, you may believe (or fear) that money will always be a hard topic in marriage—that there's no such thing as healthy conflict. If you're married, you may feel less than confident about your ability to work as a team and to agree on how to handle your money. But remember, when you can talk openly with someone, you *can* address and solve the problem. What you need are some new skills to help you: new ways to talk about money (this book is a good place to start), a plan for your money (the Baby Steps work!), and how to do healthy conflict with others (it really *is* possible). Just because money was unstable growing up doesn't mean it has to stay that way. You can learn how to do money and conflict in healthy—and calm—ways.

Apathy. Growing up in the Unstable Classroom can lead some to become apathetic about communicating about money— and even apathetic to money itself. Because of the high tension and fighting you grew up in, you may have decided to throw in the towel. You might find yourself saying, "What's the use in trying? We just end up fighting, and it never gets any better." Or maybe you decided money isn't worth the stress, and you've struck an ostrich pose with your head buried deep in the sand. If you're married, maybe you say to your spouse, "I don't care. If that's what you want to do, do it." Consciously or unconsciously, you've decided that speaking your mind would cause conflict, and the pain of conflict isn't worth it to you. Please hear me: Don't settle for the status quo! Don't give up. You have goals worth achieving. You have a life worth living, not just surviving. But it means you have to engage, really learn how to take control of your money, and put in the work.

CHAPTER 3

Calm Money Classrooms

Next up are the emotionally *calm* money quadrants: Unaware (emotionally calm and verbally closed) and Secure (emotionally calm and verbally open). If you didn't recognize your childhood experience in Quadrants 1 or 2, chances are you'll land in either Quadrant 3 or 4.

QUADRANT 3: UNAWARE CLASSROOM
Emotionally Calm and Verbally Closed

If you grew up in the Unaware Classroom, you probably didn't worry about money. In fact, you might not have even thought about money at all. Some say ignorance is bliss. And while that could be true for some things, it's definitely not true when it comes to money. To make wise decisions with money, you have to know the whole picture—the good, the bad, and the ugly. I hope you're all nodding in agreement with me, but if you grew up in the Unaware Classroom, you may not know where to begin to look at the whole picture.

Being raised in a household where no one ever talked about money is very common, but unlike the Anxious Classroom, those in the Unaware Classroom felt like life was all good. Everything seemed totally fine. You had no idea the state of your parents' money situation and didn't have to worry about it. Maybe your family was well-off but didn't talk about money around the kids. Or maybe your parents struggled, but they didn't appear to worry about it (and maybe they really weren't worried about it). Either way, the kids had no idea how money worked. You either believed there was plenty of money, or money wasn't even on your radar.

Some parents created this type of money classroom because they didn't want their kids to worry. They didn't want to put adult stress or responsibility on their children. Personal finance was just that—personal—and it was for adults to handle. Their motivation to protect was good even if it left their kids in the dark. And while it's very important for parents to share the principles of money in age-appropriate ways with their children, parents in this category often shared nothing or almost nothing with their kids.

Some families fall into this quadrant because of the dynamic between parents. Maybe one parent spent more money than they had, and the other kept quiet to maintain the peace. Or one parent was completely in charge of the money, and the other parent had no clue they were in debt. The environment appeared peaceful because there wasn't open conflict around money—when the reality was finances were difficult.

This type of environment reminds me of a group of people on a party boat without a captain. Everyone is having a great time and enjoying the sunset, but no one knows where they're going. No one's leading, and no one wants to. Why rock the boat with questions and start giving directions? Everyone is happy, so let's just let the good times roll. Meanwhile, the boat is drifting and no one even cares.

But at some point, someone on that boat needs to have a conversation about where the boat is going! Are there enough supplies? Who will take charge when a storm comes? What about food? Everyone just assumes someone will take care of all of it, but it's never talked about. In the same way, your parents may have communicated about money, but you never heard it. Or one parent assumed the other had things under control, and they never discussed it.

One of my friends described her childhood to me as "bliss." She wasn't spoiled, but she never felt like she was lacking. There was always plenty of everything. There were always birthday gifts and presents under the tree at Christmas. There were always vacations. She thought everything was fine. But as a married adult with her own child, she began to put the pieces together. As it turns out, her parents aren't actually in a good place financially. They have very little retirement savings and lots of credit card debt. Her mom recently told her she would always put Christmas expenses on a credit card, and her dad never knew she was accumulating debt. This realization shattered the picture in her head of her parents' financial health and was a hard Milestone Moment for my friend.

Coming face-to-face with your parents' weaknesses is unnerving. It's a hard place for any of us to be. But I am so proud of the recent conversations my friend has had with her parents, encouraging them to take control of their money. She could be the catalyst for change in her parents' financial turnaround.

Challenges for Quadrant 3: Unaware Classroom

Feeling Betrayed. Growing up in Quadrant 3, you may feel betrayed because your parents didn't teach you how to handle money. Or like my friend, you might have discovered that the calm, secure feeling you had about your parents' financial health was completely false. Maybe your parents kept the truth from you. This reality might now have you questioning everything you learned from them. It would be completely normal to feel angry or hurt. And it's possible you might need to work through some of those things with a professional counselor.

I have a coworker who grew up in the Unaware Classroom, and as an adult, she asked her parents why they shared so little with her about money. Her dad thought for a moment and quietly responded, "I told you far more about money than my dad ever told me. I thought it was enough." Can you hear the sincerity in that statement? He really believed he was doing the best for his daughter. I'm not excusing away the mistakes of the past, but I do want you to hear a parent's perspective. As a mom myself, I have a lot of empathy for parents. I'm nowhere near perfect, but I really am trying to do what's best for my children. And I think there's value in recognizing when your parents were doing their best—even if it fell short. It doesn't right any wrongs, but it can help ease the sting of the pain you feel.

Right-Sizing Your Sense of Responsibility. If you find out your parents are in financial trouble, there's often a desire to rush in and help. You want to pay their mortgage for them so they don't lose their house or pay off a car loan so their vehicle isn't repossessed. Or you may want to swoop in and tell them everything they need to be doing right this minute. If you face a situation like this, I want you to take a deep breath and ask yourself what your role is as their adult child. Is it your responsibility to bail them out? To pay off their debt or keep creditors from breathing down their neck? Is it your job to coach them financially and hold them accountable? We'll discuss this in greater detail later, but the answer is no. *The financial health of other people is not your responsibility—even when you love them dearly.* Yes, you want the best for them. And it's true that their financial situation will end up affecting you on some level at some point in your life. (That's why it's important to have healthy, honest conversations with your parents. These conversations can even end up being the catalyst for change!) But own the fact that you are not responsible for their actions.

Behaving Responsibly. Another challenge you might face growing up in this classroom is sheer ignorance. It's not that you're unable to take control of your finances; it's that you don't know what you don't know. Your own finances may not have ever been on your radar. If you've never been taught how to do a proper budget, you usually don't just intuitively know why it's important and how it can help you achieve your goals. Don't beat yourself up for what you didn't know. Just begin taking steps toward controlling your money from here on out.

If you grew up in this quadrant, you might also have a habit of avoiding your finances altogether. This is kind of like the little kid who closes her eyes and sticks her fingers in her ears. You just don't want to think about it. You may spend money and push any thought of consequences out of your mind. If you're married, you might be tempted to let your spouse handle everything. But this is a dangerous way to live for a lot of reasons.

If this is you, I'm going to offer you a little tough love for a moment: It's not okay to ignore your money anymore. It's not okay to spend your money and hope for the best. In order to change your financial life, you have to be willing to face your budget. If you don't have a budget, you need to create one today. In chapter 14, I've included my favorite places to go for simple, practical help with money no matter where you're starting from. But if you don't have a budget, start with that. You can download our free EveryDollar budgeting app, and it will walk you through how to set up your zero-based budget in less than ten minutes. Making a change may be really uncomfortable at first—because change can be hard—but it will be worth it! Your money and your life will thank you for it!

Pressing into Conflict. If your childhood household avoided conflict, any type of conflict may feel *really* uncomfortable to you. You may have a hard time initiating hard conversations with others. You may prefer keeping the peace over talking to your spouse about a purchase you don't agree with. Or if you feel like a friend took advantage of your generosity, you may choose to keep quiet. But listen: Few people enjoy conflict for the sake of conflict. And in order to grow and do what's best for your money situation, these uncomfortable conversations are necessary.

If you're in an abusive relationship, it might not be okay to talk about hard things (unless a third party is present, like a mediator or counselor). Otherwise, you need to know it really *is* okay to talk about hard things. It's okay for it to be uncomfortable. In fact, it's good and necessary to stand up for what's right for you. Having good boundaries makes you healthy—not a bad person. What would truly be bad is to spend your whole life going with the flow, never speaking up, and never getting what you need.

Practicing Transparency. If you didn't grow up with parents who talked about money, it can be difficult to know how to talk about money with your kids. How do you do this part of parenting well? What should you share? How much should you share and when? I've got good news that can take some of the pressure off: Your example is huge. As you take control and keep control of your money, you'll have a lot of opportunities over the years to model good money habits. Use these opportunities to talk openly about why your family makes certain choices with money. Just keep it age appropriate. If you need more help with this, my dad and I wrote a whole book on the subject called *Smart Money Smart Kids.* It will give you a lot of practical ways to raise money-smart kids.

QUADRANT 4: SECURE CLASSROOM
Emotionally Calm and Verbally Open

Quadrant 4, the Secure Classroom, is the ideal money classroom. Emotionally calm and verbally open environments aren't perfect, but they do reflect homes where parents practice healthy money habits and where kids feel the most safe and secure. Money doesn't cause stress, because the parents know how to manage it well and are in control. If you grew up in this classroom, your parent or parents talked about money often and openly. There was calm, intentional decision-making around money. Maybe you witnessed budget meetings or budget date nights. It wasn't always easy, but those meetings were productive. There was mutual respect between your parents, and they were connected and on the same page. They may have even brought you in on some of the budgeting decisions or asked you to be a part of the discussion.

Let me point out here that your parents didn't have to have a lot of money to be in the Secure Classroom. There may not have been a ton of money, but they were managing what they had well. One of my friends from college recalls that her childhood was exactly like this. Her parents told her no often, but it wasn't out of stress—it was out of discipline and good judgment. They were intentionally getting out of debt, and they included her and her siblings on the journey. As a family, they celebrated the progress they made along the way. By the time she graduated high school, her parents had saved enough money to help her with college and even started a small mutual fund for her. They didn't live in the nicest house or drive expensive cars, but what they had, they owned. She had watched them create—and stick to—a budget, so she learned that when you have a plan, you're in control of your money.

Her Milestone Moment was the day she moved into the dorm her freshman year of college. She was so excited to meet her roommate for the first time! It was hot and stressful that day as hundreds of people navigated the hallways with loads of boxes and pillows and piles of clothes. After she and her roommate were introduced, her roommate's parents began talking about money as they unpacked boxes. The mood in the room changed almost instantly from excitement to anxiety.

She couldn't help but listen as the couple's conversation escalated. They were openly disrespectful to each other as they bickered about how much was appropriate to spend on curtains for the dorm room window. Finally, with the argument left unresolved, her roommate's mom just walked out. Her dad handed his credit card to her roommate and said, "Here, take this. I'll just worry about it when the bill comes. But do *not* tell your mom." In three minutes flat my friend realized how differently she'd grown up—and how thankful she was to have grown up in the Secure Classroom.

Challenges for Quadrant 4: Secure Classroom

Underestimating All It Takes. Now, we know having money-smart parents is huge, but it doesn't mean you'll automatically end up money-smart too. You don't get a pass on your own hard work. Growing up in this quadrant doesn't mean healthy attitudes about money are going to come easily to you. You probably didn't see *all* of the conversations your parents had around money or what they sacrificed to take control of their money. You probably didn't hear about the car your dad *really* wanted when he paid cash for the reliable-but-used minivan instead. You didn't know about the vacation your mom really wanted to take that summer. You only knew that you had a blast on that family camping trip when you were in elementary school.

Growing up in this classroom, you missed at least some of the pain and discipline your parents experienced saying no to things they wanted to have or do. It took a lot of work and sacrifice to raise you in this quadrant. Now it's your turn to do the same thing for your family. But you're going to have to be every bit as disciplined and focused as your parents were to manage your own money well.

Feeling Entitled. In the same way that you can't expect to get a pass on the hard work, you also can't expect your standard of living to automatically be the same as your parents. Radio personality Larry Burkett used to say that couples spend the first five to seven years of their marriage trying to attain the same standard of living as their parents—only it took their parents thirty-five years to get there.[2] This can be true no matter which classroom you grew up in. But as graduates of the Secure Classroom, remember your parents worked hard to get where they are. So it will take time for you to get there too. Unrealistic expectations can be incredibly harmful. You can't have any sense of entitlement or bide your time waiting for a handout. You have to be ready to work hard and say no to some things you want right now. If you do, you'll be able to control your money and build a solid financial future.

MOVING QUADRANTS

As you think through your childhood and what you learned about money, keep in mind your quadrant might have changed like mine did. There are a lot of reasons for this. It could be the household income level changed or your parents got divorced or married. Or maybe they went to *Financial Peace University* and learned how to budget and get out of debt. If your money classroom changed during your childhood, you'll want to think through how each quadrant impacted you. You may also find it helpful to talk to your parents about what those earliest years were like. You might be surprised by what you learn.

YOUR CHILDHOOD DOES *NOT* DEFINE YOU

The four classrooms provide a foundation for understanding why you handle money the way you do and the challenges you may face. It also gives you insight into the people closest to you. But you know what it doesn't do? It doesn't define you.

Global researcher and thought leader Marcus Buckingham said, "Childhood either enables you or stunts you; it doesn't create you."[3] Your childhood may have given you a rocky start, but it doesn't make or break you. Regardless of the household you grew up in, you get to choose your quadrant from this point forward. Does our childhood affect us and shape us? Absolutely. But at Ramsey Solutions, we've seen millions of families move to the Secure Classroom no matter their circumstance—and that's what I want for you too. People who came from the worst financial households decided to do something different. They changed their lives, and so can you.

NOW IT'S YOUR TURN

At the end of each section I've designed a series of questions called "Now It's Your Turn" to help you think through what we've covered and how it applies to you. Now, I know some of you will be tempted to skip this part. But I encourage you to read through each one and take your time writing down your answers. At the end of the book, we'll circle back to what you wrote to put your insights into action.

1. Which money classroom did you grow up in? How do you know?
2. Write down your Milestone Moments and what they taught you about money.
3. If you're married, talk to your spouse about the different quadrants and find out which one they grew up in. Discuss the similarities and differences between your money classrooms and how they affect your money choices and relationship today.
4. If you're not already functioning in a Secure Classroom with your own finances, what should you do differently to get there? Do you know anyone who's currently in a Secure household? If so, ask them to explain how they manage their money.
5. Imagine you're living in a Secure Classroom. Write down some thoughts and emotions you feel around having openness and peace when it comes to your money. Creating a Secure Classroom is a process, so don't get discouraged when it takes some time!

CHAPTER 4

Your Unique Money Tendencies

The snow crunched under our feet as we walked through the freezing night in Crested Butte, Colorado. If you've never been to Crested Butte, just picture the most magical, charming ski town ever. We were there for our annual family vacation. There were seven of us that night, walking down streets lined with shops and restaurants, talking and laughing. Christmas lights were strung in all the trees. It was so picturesque and felt like we'd walked onto the set of a Hallmark Christmas movie.

Soon we came to the restaurant. We'd be eating sushi—a family favorite—and were in high spirits because we'd heard rave reviews about the place. When we walked in the front door, we had to go down a flight of stairs into what seemed like the basement. But when we got to the bottom of the stairs and walked through the doorway, it was like being transported to Japan. The ambience was vibrant, and the restaurant was packed. The hostess sat us in a corner booth with a large round table so all seven adults could sit together. As we took off our jackets and got settled, I could tell it was going to be a good night.

We got quiet as we all began looking over the menu, trying to narrow down the endless options. Then Dad said, "Let's just order a bunch of sushi rolls to share!" We all liked that idea, so he took a poll of the table, asking for our favorites, and we shouted out different ideas. When the waitress came, Dad ordered way more rolls than the seven of us could ever eat. After the server took our massive order, my mom waved her over. I couldn't hear what they were saying, but Mom was pointing to the menu and the server was nodding and writing something on her note-pad. When she left, I asked my mom what that was all about. Her response still makes me laugh. She said, "I ordered my own salmon rolls." We all looked at her with blank stares.

"Mom! We just ordered enough food to feed a small country! If somehow we run out, you can always order more!"

But her mind was made up. "I want the salmon rolls. You all always eat those first, and I don't want any of the others. So I got my own."

There was silence around the table. Mom was smiling the whole time. She had her own rolls coming, and no one was going to eat them.

We still tease her about those salmon rolls to this day. But when I look back at that moment, I'm reminded that each of us sees life differently. We each have our own tendencies, and though we may not spend much time thinking about it, those tendencies carry over into our decisions about money. We've all gone out to dinner with friends. And when it comes time to pay the bill some people in the group are great with splitting the check evenly, while others at the table are cringing because they just want to pay for their order. It can sometimes get a little awkward. But the thing is, it's okay that everyone may want to do it differently—because we're all wired differently. My mom wanting her own sushi is a classic example of a scarcity mindset versus an abundance mindset (a money tendency we'll talk about shortly). Neither one is right or wrong—they're just different ways of seeing the world.

After talking with thousands of people, I've noticed seven major money tendencies we all have. In this chapter, we'll break those down so you can get a better grasp of how you're uniquely wired to spend (or not spend) money. The seven money tendencies are:

1. Saver or Spender
2. Nerd or Free Spirit
3. Experiences or Things
4. Quality or Quantity
5. Safety or Status
6. Abundance or Scarcity
7. Planned Giving or Spontaneous Giving

Keep in mind that these tendencies are specific to how we deal with money, and I'm presenting them as either/or. Don't overthink this part. You might be somewhere in between too. It's a *scale*. You're wired to think and act in certain ways, and while none of the tendencies are right or wrong, they do have implications. Understanding how these tendencies affect you will help you make progress on your financial goals faster.

While you're thinking through where you fall on each scale, also consider the people in your life closest to you and how they're wired. If you're married, pay close attention. The saying "opposites attract" can be pretty spot on. If you find yourself on one side of a scale, there's a good chance your spouse is on the opposite side. You might be surprised, so get ready! At the end of the chapter, there's an opportunity for you to write down your tendencies and the tendencies of those closest to you.

TENDENCY #1: SAVER OR SPENDER

We're going to start with an easy one. The first major money tendency we're going to look at is saver or spender. Imagine someone gave you a hundred dollars. What's the very first thing you think to do with that money? I'm looking for your natural response. Sometimes our experiences with money as adults can complicate our reaction to this question. So for this scale, think about your instinctive response to the question. Thinking about what you would have done as a child might help.

If you're a *saver*, your first instinct would be to save that hundred dollars. Savers prefer to have money tucked away. There's a ten-year-old in my neighborhood who told me she has $200 stashed away "just in case" something happens. That makes me smile because it just goes to show that savers manifest this behavior early on. Saving money comes naturally to them. Putting money away for the future isn't a major sacrifice; it gives them a sense of security. They're patient and willing to wait. Like spenders, some savers love to find deals and use coupons—but it's all with the purpose of saving for the future.

For the natural *spender*, just the idea of that hundred-dollar gift unleashed the creative possibilities of what could be purchased with that money. You remember that old cliché "money burns a hole in your pocket"? That's how spenders feel: They can't wait to use that extra money when they have it. Spending money is easy. But saving? Not always. Now, spenders can sometimes get a bad rap—I know, because I am one! We can be labeled "irresponsible," but that's not always the case. The desire to spend money is not the same as a lack of responsibility or a lack of control. Spenders can be very disciplined. I love to spend money and have no shame about it—and I'm also very good with a budget. The two are not mutually exclusive.

What's dangerous for spenders and savers both is going to the extremes. This is true of every scale we'll look at. As a spender, if you spend *everything* you make, you're going to be broke. And, savers, if you save *everything* you make, you're going to miss out on a lot of fun experiences that make life worth living. This is pretty obvious when we think about it—but the point is, we *need* to think about it.

Tackling the *why* behind *how* we handle our money is sometimes as simple as recognizing our natural behaviors and making small adjustments to our choices throughout the day. Here's an example: I'm a spender, and I love pizza. I was ordering pizza online for dinner recently and, without really thinking, just loaded my shopping cart with several different pizzas that sounded good in the moment. When I clicked "Checkout" and saw my total, it was a little over fifty dollars, and that didn't include a tip for the delivery driver!

Now I *seriously* love pizza, but that was way more than I wanted to spend on dinner that night for just me and my husband. So instead of mindlessly clicking on the "Order Now" button, I went back through my cart, removed some items, and cut my total in half. It took less than thirty seconds, and that small choice saved us twenty-five dollars. As you think through where you fall on this scale and the ones to come, remember: Sometimes all it takes is being aware of your tendencies so you can make different choices that will make a big impact over time.

TENDENCY #2: NERD OR FREE SPIRIT

My dad coined the phrase "Nerd or Free Spirit" years ago to describe the two different approaches to budgeting. It was funny and 100 percent accurate and quickly became part of our everyday vocabulary at Ramsey Solutions. But I'm using these terms here to describe a person's overall approach to money—not just to budgeting.

No doubt you'll find yourself relating easily to one over the other because they're pretty opposite.

When I'm speaking to large groups, I'll often ask for a show of hands for who in the audience is a nerd and who is a free spirit. The audience's response is always so telling. Nerds will raise their hands precisely and knowingly nod their heads. But when I ask who the free spirits are in the room, they cheer and shout. They will literally start the wave sometimes! It always makes for a funny moment because there's no way you can mistake the two.

Alright, nerds, let's start with you. You know you're a *nerd* if you read the instruction manuals to any new product. Punctuality is important to you. Your socks are neatly folded in the drawer. You read the introductions in books. Your tax return is prepared for the dreaded April 15 deadline well in advance. These nerd behaviors aren't just in your everyday life either. They define your finances too. You love being in control of your money. You like things buttoned up and orderly. Nerds tend to be naturally proactive with budgeting and intentional about where their money goes. If you don't have a budget already, the idea of one appeals to you. Nerds can make a lot of progress with their money quickly because they create a plan and love sticking to it. They're laser-focused on what they need to do to win with money, and they're on top of the details and decisions.

Just like with the saver vs. spender scale, there are unhealthy extremes for nerds to watch out for. Nerds, be careful you don't become legalistic. Sometimes you can live and die by the rules and the budget, and you end up wearing yourself and your family out. Nerds can also be guilty of withholding grace when money mistakes happen. (And they will happen!) This can be withholding grace from themselves or from their spouse or family member. Nerds have also been known to be uptight. Ahem. And if things aren't going according to plan, it can really throw them off. But I love nerds! My husband, Winston, is a nerd, and I so love his attention to detail and how he always knows exactly what's going on. Nerds, you are awesome.

Okay, free spirits, it's your turn. You know you're a *free spirit* when you view instruction manuals as coasters. You consult them only if you get really stuck and can't figure it out on your own. You *try* to be on time, but hey, sometimes fashionably late works. Your closet isn't terribly organized. You definitely skipped the introduction to this book, because let's just get to the good stuff, right? And, wait, Tax Day is when? If this sounds more like you, you're probably a free spirit.

When it comes to money, free spirits tend to say, "Everything is going to be fine. It will all work out!" You have a "let's enjoy life" mentality. Just reading the word *budget* in the previous paragraphs about nerds made you break out in hives. And the idea of being detailed and restricted with money seems boring and way too controlled. You'll do it, but it's not your favorite. Listen, I'm a free spirit. I totally get it! Here's the thing: We know how to enjoy life. There's not a lot that stresses us out, and that can be a really helpful perspective to have. We live every day with a sense of carefree excitement, which allows experiences to happen that might not otherwise happen. That might not be easy to cram into a spreadsheet, but it has a lot of value. Plus, we can easily see the big picture behind something like a budget and remember why we're doing it in the first place.

But if we're not careful, free spirits, we can fall into unhealthy extremes too. We can be a little too sloppy. Details don't always come naturally to a free spirit, so we can miss deadlines and important information—and some of those things can be costly. I joked about Tax Day, but missing that deadline can cost thousands of dollars in penalties if we don't know what's going on. We can overlook critical things like life insurance and having a will. We can miss due dates for bills and not even be aware of the mess we're creating. If we're not intentional about our money, we can be the ones who look up in a few years and wonder where on earth it all went.

Before we move on, we need to clear up a big misconception about nerds and free spirits. A lot of people think that all nerds are savers and all free spirits are spenders. This isn't true. You can definitely be a nerd who loves to spend money or a free spirit who loves to save money. It's true that Winston is a nerd-saver and I'm a free spirit-spender, but my parents are the opposite. People would never guess it, but my mom is a free spirit-saver and my dad is a nerd-spender. *Surprise!* You can be a master budgeter and still find it easy to buy stuff. And you can be a reluctant budgeter and naturally hold tight to your cash. So you'll need to think through both areas to figure out which one you are.

TENDENCY #3: EXPERIENCES OR THINGS

The next major money tendency we're going to explore is what you prefer to buy: experiences or things. Just for fun, let's compare Winston's favorite Christmas gift from a few years ago and my favorite Christmas gift. I'm not even joking when I tell you he asked for an adult-sized scooter. He wanted one so he could ride alongside our then four-year-old daughter Amelia while she scooted around on her pink scooter. I laughed when he put it on his list, and then his whole family laughed when he opened it on Christmas. But now that I've ridden it, I get it. It's actually a blast! So I no longer hate on his scooter game.

What do you think my favorite gift was? It was a gift card to my favorite spa. I was thrilled because I love experiences, and I couldn't wait to de-stress with a relaxing massage. If I have extra money to spend, I'll spend it on dinner with friends, going to the movies, or traveling. I value *experiences* and Winston values tangible *things*.

People on opposite sides of this scale don't always understand each other. Winston doesn't spend money on experiences. He laughs at how much I can spend on an hour-long massage when the same amount would buy a nice pair of shoes I could wear for years. And that totally makes sense if you value things! But as an "experience person," I'd rather walk away with a memory than a physical item. Winston spends money on things like new camping supplies, headphones, or gadgets. And while those things don't necessarily mean a lot to me, he gets a lot of enjoyment from buying things that make his life better. They're both equally valid preferences.

If you're married, this is a great conversation to have. Ask your spouse if they'd rather have an experience or a thing. For so long, Winston and I never talked about this. It's not that I feared it would cause conflict. I just never understood why he didn't want to drop some money to go out to a nice restaurant. After we figured this out, it helped us in our budgeting *and* our communication. So think about how you like to spend extra money. Do you love experiences or things?

TENDENCY #4: QUALITY OR QUANTITY

The next major money tendency to consider is quality or quantity. Would you rather have one high-quality item that will last for years or several lower-quality options to choose from? Some people prefer spending money on a quality item, while others enjoy the variety that quantity brings.

QUALITY ← → **QUANTITY**

For instance, say a quality pair of shoes costs a hundred dollars. Would you prefer one pair of those, two pairs of fifty-dollar shoes, or even five pairs of twenty-dollar shoes? Or if you're an experience person, think back to our hundred-dollar gift example. Did you dream of buying a hundred-dollar adventure with that money, or did you see yourself spreading the love around on several activities?

If you lean toward *quality*, you want things that are more likely to last. You'll happily save up to buy a nicer product, which in turn will give you long-lasting value. You are also more likely to take care of your things, because they're higher quality. I find that people who lean more toward quality will research and plan their purchases beforehand. Quality spenders do not tend to be impulse shoppers.

The unhealthy extreme for quality buyers is to buy expensive things in order to impress other people or to make yourself feel superior to others because of what you own. You can also fall into a pattern where you only buy "the best" out of habit. Like you've only ever bought one brand of pricey makeup when there are less expensive options you would actually like—but you've just never thought about it. I encourage you to really consider your purchases. Ask yourself if it's really necessary or if there's a less expensive option out there that you would enjoy just as much. You could be pleasantly surprised by what you find—and be able to save extra money toward one of your goals.

If you value *quantity*, you probably enjoy the creativity and possibility that variety offers. You like having ten options versus going back to the same item over and over. People who lean toward quantity are often great bargain shoppers. They pride themselves on the art of finding a great deal. At their least healthy, quantity buyers may find they shop in an effort to get the "high" that comes from either having a lot or making a purchase. That high always wears off, but the money is gone by that point.

For me, I've changed over the years. When I was younger, I was all quantity all the way. I would go to the mall with thirty dollars and somehow come home with ten different items! I loved to shop and loved buying a lot of different things. Now, I'm more in the center of the quantity and quality scale.

I've also found a preference for quality over quantity in specific areas. In accessories, for instance, I have a few sentimental jewelry pieces that are high quality, but the majority of my jewelry accessories are fun earrings and statement necklaces that cost twenty dollars or less. And if they go out of style, I don't feel guilty getting rid of them. Other places in my life, I prefer quality over quantity. Take purses, for example. I've learned I beat my purses up—and inevitably, old crumbled-up Goldfish crackers end up at the bottom (thanks to my kids!)—so I prefer one that will hold up to hard use. I don't need or want ten different purses to choose from. A purse for me is more of an investment piece. Quantity isn't important. Instead, I'll spend more for a quality item.

I recently played the 30-Day Minimalism Game from The Minimalists, Joshua Fields Millburn and Ryan Nicodemus, and it shifted me even more toward the middle of the quality vs. quantity scale. The idea is that you give away, throw away, or sell the number of items corresponding to the date on the calendar. So if it's March 10, then you give, sell, or throw away ten items by midnight that day. The challenge is to do this every day for a whole month.

I have to tell you, it was incredible. I got rid of over 500 items! It turns out there were a lot of things in my house we didn't use or need as a family—clothes, jewelry, food in the pantry, random items in the closets, and toys in the kids' playroom. And I discovered that the less clutter I have in the house, the smoother my life is. I no longer stand in my closet sorting through a bunch of hangers to figure out what to wear, because now I have far fewer clothes. I waste less time now. It has really helped me, and I'm enjoying having fewer things. If you struggle with overdoing it on quantity like me, consider taking The Minimalists' challenge to give you a different perspective. Also, reflect on past purchases you've made that you've regretted because the product didn't last. Doing so will help you start to see what items you prefer to be quality rather than quantity.

TENDENCY #5: SAFETY OR STATUS

The fifth money tendency to consider is whether you want money for safety or status. On a basic level, money is the currency that allows us to buy food, pay bills, and keep gas in the car. Without money, we would be stuck and unable to go anywhere or do anything. But go a little deeper than this basic level. What does money mean to you below the surface? Why do you want to have money? What's your motivation? In my work, I've discovered that most of us associate money with either safety or status.

If money is about *safety* for you, you want to know with as much assurance as possible that you'll be okay if something hard and unexpected happens. You find comfort in knowing you can financially absorb whatever curve ball life throws at you:

- This month's bills? You have a budget and know you can cover all of your expenses.
- Laid off from your job? You can depend on your six months of expenses saved in an emergency fund.
- Scary medical emergency? You've got health insurance and the money to choose the care that's right for you.
- God forbid, your spouse unexpectedly passes away? You both have a will in place and life insurance that will cover a large portion of the costs of raising your kids.

For people concerned about safety, having money is all about having *peace of mind.*

If you're a "safety person," you want to watch out for living in fear. This is especially true if you've experienced something traumatic in your past. As you make money decisions, make sure you're seeing and considering all of the possibilities, not just defaulting to the least risky choice. There are people who could go out right now and buy anything they want, but they won't allow themselves to because they're so fearful of the unknown. They have allowed fear to control how they spend money. If you struggle with this, it's important to recognize the fear and push yourself outside your comfort zone (in responsible ways). If you've worn a hole in your go-to pair of shoes, it's entirely appropriate to budget for and buy yourself a new pair! Don't allow fear to keep you from using and enjoying the money you've worked for and saved.

The other end of this scale is status. If money is about *status* for you, it's how you measure your success. Think of a scorecard. It's easy to see you're winning by the number of tick marks out to the side. Money—and what it can buy—are those tick marks: the type of home you live in, the activities you're involved in, getting to go on that dream vacation. Money is used as a benchmark that enhances your life. For "status people," having money is all about *personal achievement*.

Now, this doesn't have to be shallow or negative. If the tick marks on your status scorecard include seeing wealth as a responsibility to manage well and to give away to help others, you've got a healthy perspective. But you should be on the lookout because it can be a slippery slope. If you're more into status like I am, you can get off track if your achievements become more important than your character or the people around you. If climbing the social ladder, living in an expensive home, and driving the coolest car become the most important things to you, honestly, you're going to be disappointed. It might be fun, but it won't make you happy or satisfy you for a lifetime.

As someone who is wired as more of a status seeker, I know I have to stay in check and make sure both the stuff I own and the money I make don't define me as a person. A larger bank account doesn't make anyone a better, more important person. The truth is that money is just a magnifying glass: It makes you more of whoever you are. If you're kind and generous, you'll be even more kind and generous with money. If you're rude and self-centered, you'll be even more rude and self-centered with money. Money is just a tool and has nothing to do with your identity. Who you are and who you're becoming has little to do with what you're achieving.

One other word of caution: Be sure you're intentionally choosing what success looks like for you, not just absorbing what others think. Culture feeds us a steady diet of what it believes is important. (We'll cover that in chapter 9.) If we're not careful, we can spend years working toward something that ends up meaning nothing to us. Be sure you're living the life *you* want—not what other people prescribe for you or think you need.

TENDENCY #6: ABUNDANCE OR SCARCITY

The next major money tendency we're going to explore is the abundance or scarcity scale. This goes back to the beginning of the chapter with my mom's sushi order. Knowing where you are on this scale will tell you *a lot* about why you make the money decisions you do.

People who lean toward *abundance* believe there's always more than enough for everyone. There will always be more opportunities, more relationships, more money, and more options. They have a glass-half-full mentality. When challenges come along, they tend to say, "It'll all work out." Or something like, "This hard thing is really an opportunity!" They tend to take more risks and generally don't fear the outcome of a decision. After all, if they don't like the outcome, they can just make another decision. There are endless decisions, right? Those with an abundance mentality are willing to do things others might not do. They take risks more easily and usually have a high tolerance for change. They also tend to be natural givers, believing there are always ways to make more money.

What's tricky for abundance-minded people is they can become so optimistic that they stop walking in wisdom. I have a friend who interned for a nonprofit one summer during college. She was passionate about the people and their mission and felt moved to quietly give her entire salary back to the organization. Though her motives were pure, she didn't talk to anyone about her decision before making it, and she didn't really think through the consequences of it. She ended up giving all of the money (after taxes) back to the nonprofit and returned to school that fall with zero savings.

Those with an abundance mindset need to be careful to count the cost of their choices before they make a decision. What can feel like big faith is sometimes the absence of wisdom. In this case, her generosity put her in an unhealthy financial position. If you're an abundance person, make sure you're not making important decisions in a vacuum. Instead, be sure to seek counsel. Proverbs 11:14 (NKJV) says, "In the multitude of counselors there is safety."

Those on the other end of the scale have a *scarcity* mindset. They make money decisions based on a belief that resources are finite. There's a limit to them. To scarcity folks, the glass is half empty. They tend to hold on to possessions more tightly because "they might need that someday" and don't want to be wasteful. They sometimes fear losing things because they might not be able to replace them. Overall, those with a scarcity mentality tend to play it safer with money—which often makes them very wise. They're typically less wasteful with money because, to them, it's a limited resource. They're often more careful, thoughtful, and intentional with their finances. They're always prepared and count the cost before moving forward with a decision. Our scarcity friends can be wonderfully realistic and objective about opportunities because they don't get swept up in best-case scenarios.

An unhealthy scarcity mindset, however, is very different. An unhealthy scarcity mindset ultimately believes there isn't enough and won't ever be enough. It's a mindset that believes God can't or won't provide for them—that there are limits to God's goodness and ability. If they get rid of that extra set of dishes in the garage, and then one day need another set, they believe they won't have enough money to buy more. People with an unhealthy scarcity mindset make decisions about their money and stuff based on fear, not facts. They too often miss smart financial opportunities that will move them forward in life because they've allowed fear to cloud their thinking.

If you struggle with an unhealthy scarcity mindset, there are a couple of things you can do. First, don't rely solely on your own opinion when it comes to your money. Seek out wise counsel and listen to what they say. Like if you need help investing, check out our SmartVestor Pros. They have the heart of a teacher and will help guide you to the best ways to grow your money. If you need help with things like getting out of debt, creating a budget, or avoiding bankruptcy, contact a Ramsey Financial Coach. An objective third party will be able to give you a helpful perspective for your situation.

Another way to combat an unhealthy scarcity mindset is to give more. Now, I know it sounds crazy to give something away when you already think you don't have enough. But giving is one of the most powerful things you'll ever do to help unlock an untrusting heart. We'll talk more in depth about giving in chapter 12. For now, start with something small. What do you have right now that you could give away to bless someone else? A clothing item you don't wear? A loaf of fresh bread that you baked? A larger-than-normal tip at a restaurant? Commit to giving away something small every week for a month and see how it begins to shift your thinking.

TENDENCY #7: PLANNED GIVING OR SPONTANEOUS GIVING

The last major money tendency we'll look at in this chapter is how you give: Do you plan your giving, or do you give spontaneously in the moment? Again, there's no right or wrong here. We all have a natural giving tendency, and it's important to recognize and understand how you do it.

PLANNED GIVING		SPONTANEOUS GIVING

Are you quick to give? If you pass someone on the sidewalk asking for donations, do you feel compelled to give right away? If you hear of a worthy organization that's asking for a donation, do you jump to give? Then you're probably a spontaneous giver.

Are you slower to give? Or do you stop, think, and calculate before you give? Do you even need to calculate exactly what you're going to give before you give? If you answered yes, then you're a planned giver. We'll look at spontaneous givers first and then planned givers.

As a *spontaneous* giver, you like to have freedom to respond with your heart. You naturally live life with open hands, and you can't help but help. When you see a need, you try to meet it right away. So many people are helped because of spontaneous givers. If the world was made up entirely of planned givers, a lot of these opportunities would easily be missed. Plus, there's so much joy to be experienced when you live life ready to help.

If you're a spontaneous giver, make sure your giving isn't ineffective. Dropping five dollars in a bucket here and there can feel good in the moment, but it may not have the impact you think it does. Emotional giving definitely isn't wrong. I just want you to remember that if it's the only way you give, you may miss opportunities to make a larger impact.

If you're naturally a *planned* giver, you have so many strengths! Typically, planned givers take their resources and money very seriously. They don't give to every good cause they hear about because they've already decided how they're going to give and they're committed to it. They're also careful to avoid giving to individuals or nonprofits they haven't researched.

Planned giving can also help you when you get those off-the-cuff donation requests, whether it's someone at your front door trying to raise money or the cashier at the grocery store. Because you're strategic and planned in your giving, you can feel zero guilt about saying no. You can simply respond with the truth and say, "I'll look into this, but I've already decided on my giving for the month."

I naturally lean toward spontaneous giving. When I see a need, I love to rush in to help out—it's my nature. But over time, I've shifted to more of a planner mindset because I've seen how being intentional with giving can have a bigger impact. Winston and I see giving as a big responsibility, and we look at what and who we give to as closely as we do our investments. We're careful to research the organizations we want to give to, and we set a plan for how we'll give.

As good as giving is, believe it or not, it can create conflict in relationships. If you're a planned giver, you can get pretty frustrated when you see your spouse giving a few dollars at the grocery store for their charity efforts or spending money on things you don't need to support local fundraising efforts. It can even seem wasteful. And if you're a spontaneous giver, your planner spouse can seem heartless when they pass by good opportunity after good opportunity to help people in need. But giving doesn't have to be a source of friction.

After practicing this for a while, one of the things Winston and I have learned to do in our planned giving is to budget for spontaneous giving. We want to be responsible and strategic with our giving, but we also want to leave margin in our hearts and budget to help. That way, if something unexpected comes up that we feel called to give to, we can! I never deny something I feel God doing in the moment.

So if you're a planned giver, be sure to leave room for the unexpected. And regardless of your tendency, you'll need to practice grace with yourself and others. If you're married, talk to your spouse about each other's giving style and look for ways to support them. The bottom line here is that you want to be able to give generously—whether it's planned or spontaneous—so practice this in small ways *now* so you can give big in the future.

WIRED DIFFERENTLY

When you know your money tendencies and the tendencies of those around you, you're in a position to make far better decisions. Let me give you an example. Years ago, a friend of mine was car shopping with her husband. This was before they ever took *Financial Peace University* or committed to debt-free living. At the car dealership, they looked at both used cars and new cars. When her financially conservative husband said no to the used car and yes to financing a new car, she trusted he had run the numbers and done his research. *But he hadn't.* They ended up with a whopping $700 a month car payment, and a few months later, her husband was laid off from his job. You can imagine the stress they felt facing that payment every month.

Only later, after going through *Financial Peace University*, did they realize that she is the nerd and he is the free spirit. My friend assumed her husband had done his homework because that's how *she's* wired. But her free-spirited husband wanted to buy the car because of how nice it would be for her to drive. He had the best of intentions, but it wasn't a wise decision.

Fast-forward to today. Now when they buy a car, they do things differently. It's become a joint effort, and they pay with cash. They talk through what they need and want in a new vehicle. Then she runs the numbers to determine what they can afford, how long they'll need to save, and which vehicles best fit their needs. (She loves doing this!) She talks over the research with him, and he makes sure they choose something they'll actually enjoy driving. (He loves doing this!) Today they communicate differently, trust each other more, live in their strengths, and make far better decisions.

Using your money tendencies to complement your spouse's is a no-brainer. But your money tendencies can also be really helpful when you're making money decisions on your own. Remember my friend who gave away her salary one summer in college to the non-profit she was working for? If she got a do-over, she would tell her younger self to reach out to someone she trusted and talk through the different options before making a decision. She would still want to donate some of it back to the organization, but she now sees that saving a good portion of it to cover college expenses the following semester would have been wise—and given her peace of mind.

MODERATION

We've covered a lot of ground in this chapter about our money tendencies. No matter where you fall on these scales, remember: None of these tendencies are inherently right or wrong. They just show us how we're wired. Our job is to recognize what our tendencies are so we can make adjustments where we need to.

So what's the goal for each scale? Moderation. Moderation just means avoiding the extremes. For example, a scarcity mindset says resources are limited, so we should plan carefully. That's wisdom! An unhealthy scarcity mindset says there will never, ever be enough, so we shouldn't even attempt something new. That's the extreme—we're defeated before we even begin.

Here are some other examples: Nerds, you want to know your numbers and be intentional, but don't be so inflexible that there's no room for spontaneous fun in your life. People who want quality: Not *everything* has to be top-of-the-line. I'm going to bet there are some areas in your life where you would actually enjoy either more variety or the extra savings you get because you've bought something less expensive. People who love things over experiences: Don't get so focused on your next purchase that you stop connecting with others through meaningful, shared time together.

The danger of unhealthy extremes on any scale is that they hold you back. They limit your potential for growth and for really living life. Once you know your natural tendencies and their unhealthy extremes, you can make better decisions and move toward the center of each scale. If you're a natural spender, are you making healthy money decisions by following a budget and setting aside savings? If your spending is out of control and your savings account is empty, this is an area you need to work on. Listen, if you'll really work on these major money tendencies, you're going to see progress!

The more you pay attention to why you spend (or don't spend) money the way you do, the more you can course-correct when you need to. Don't put this off. In one year or five years or ten years, you're going to look back and be so, so grateful you started today.

NOW IT'S YOUR TURN

1. When it comes to how you spend and relate to money, where would you place yourself on the following scales? Put a tally mark on the line where you think you fall. For example, if you're 100 percent Spender, your mark should be on the far right. If you're a Saver, but also have some strong Spender tendencies, you would mark the line pretty close to the middle but just a smidge toward the Saver side. There's no right or wrong answer!

   Saver —————————— Spender
   Nerd —————————— Free Spirit
   Experiences —————— Things
   Quality —————————— Quantity
   Safety —————————— Status
   Abundance ————————— Scarcity
   Planned Giving ————— Spontaneous Giving

2. What steps can you take to be more moderate on any scale where you're struggling?
3. When was the last time you experienced frustration or anger over how someone else handled their money? Did it have anything to do with money tendencies?
4. Are you currently experiencing stress in a relationship due to a money tendency? If so, how could you approach it based on what you've learned?

CHAPTER 5

Your Money Fears, Part 1

A few years ago my sister-in-law, Kristen, was meeting a friend for breakfast. She was in a quaint little area of downtown Knoxville, Tennessee, where she had been hundreds of times, so this place was familiar to her and felt safe. As she walked up to the restaurant, she realized it was closed. She called her friend, and they decided to meet at her friend's apartment just a block over from the restaurant.

On her way, a man approached her and asked for a cigarette. She politely told him she didn't smoke and didn't have one. Looking agitated, he looked her up and down and started walking off. Then quickly, he turned back around and demanded she give him her purse.

She heard him clearly, but she wasn't going to just hand it over. She looked at him sternly and said, "What did you say to me?"

He said, "Give me your purse!" And as he demanded it a second time, he moved his jacket to the side and pulled out a gun. He cocked it back and repeated his words a third time.

At that point, she froze. It was like an out-of-body experi-ence. Fear ran through her, and she handed the purse over. The guy grabbed it and ran off. A few seconds later, she saw another friend across the street and ran over to him for help. They called the police, and she ended up going to the police station to give a description of the man.

This was one of the scariest moments of her life, but she handled it really well. We've all experienced moments, however, when fear makes it hard to make good decisions. Real fear makes it difficult to think clearly, to process information rationally. It leads us to act when we shouldn't and not act when we should. Remember the beginning of the coronavirus pandemic in 2020? What was the first thing people began hoarding for a respiratory virus? Toilet paper. *Toilet paper?* What were we thinking? And that's the thing about fear: It stops us from thinking rationally.

Money fears are no different. Believe it or not, every single one of us either has or has had fears about money. In fact, studies show that not having enough money is one of the top ten things Americans fear most.[4] It doesn't matter how much money you have or make, everyone has experienced fear about money.

When I say *fear,* I don't mean concern or worry. I'm talking about the kind of fear that wakes you up at one o'clock in the morning in a sweat with your heart racing. The kind of fear you can't shake off. The kind that's all-consuming. It takes over your thoughts during the day, making it hard to focus on anything else. Fear like this holds you hostage because you just lost your job, and you've got three young kids to feed, a mortgage to pay, and nothing in savings. It's real and it's terrifying.

Most of us don't associate fear with anything positive, but the interesting thing about fear is that it's actually a gift. We need it. Fear is a basic, universal human emotion that protects us. It's our bodies' natural response to a perceived threat—like being held at gunpoint. Fear triggers the fight-or-flight response and tells us we need to act during dangerous circumstances. It literally and biologically motivates us. It's our bodies' way of saying, "Pay attention and *move!*" When we feel it, our bodies release hormones that sharpen our functions so we can take action.

What isn't helpful is when fear goes beyond protecting us to paralyzing us. Here's the tricky thing about it: In order for fear to protect us, it has to limit our options. I was talking with Marcus Buckingham about fear and he said, "We know what fear does to people. It narrows the mind. If you're being attacked by a tiger, you don't start thinking about the purpose of life. You just ask, 'Can I outrun the tiger?' Fear narrows the mind's focus to survival *only* and blocks out creativity." When you're walking down a sidewalk and you see a car lose control, jump the curb, and head straight for you, the only thing you need to think about is how to stay alive. Fear helps you focus in a life-and-death situation. But if you live in a *constant* state of fear, you're stuck in survival mode and can't think creatively or imagine that things could be different. Fear can help you stay alive, but it's a terrible master.

Think for a minute about money fears. What happens if you get injured in an accident and aren't able to work for three months? You're staring down twelve weeks without a single paycheck. Right at that moment—when you need *more* escape routes, *more* ways to cut expenses, *more* ways to bring in income, *more* chances for gaining ground—fear, left unchecked, will paralyze you so you can't see any options.

At its most helpful, fear can help you see the urgency of your situation and get you moving. At its least helpful, fear can block your creativity so you do nothing at all. What if Kristen didn't think quickly enough and hand over her purse? What if, instead of giving it to him right away, she'd just stood there? Who's to say that man wouldn't have done something drastic, like pull the trigger? But she stayed calm and stayed safe. In the same way, if you want to win with money, you have to acknowledge your fears and find ways to move through them.

So, how do you move through fear? At Ramsey Solutions, we do weekly staff meetings where we talk about things like new initiatives, strategy, and our core values. At a recent meeting, one of our executive vice presidents was talking about our core value of "Fear Not" and shared with us how he addresses fear in his own life. He said there are three steps:

1. Name the fear.
2. Focus on the truth.
3. Reach out for help.

The first thing to do when you're facing fear is realize it's fear. That's why you name it. When you recognize and name your fear, it can no longer lurk in the shadows, controlling your behavior without you knowing about it.

Step two is to focus on the truth. You have to go beyond naming the fear to spending time with what's true. If a child is scared to go to a new school, we spend time teaching them: It's okay to feel nervous, but you'll be safe, you'll find something you enjoy, you'll get to make new friends. And we don't just say it once—we continue to remind them so the truth sinks into their heart. The same is true for us when we're dealing with fear. We have to spend time remembering and focusing on what's really true.

And step three is to reach out for help. This means we're connecting with God and others about our fear in meaningful ways and taking action where needed. As we explore our money fears in this section, watch for how you can incorporate these three steps into your life. Second Timothy 1:7 (NKJV) says, "For God has not given us a spirit of fear, but of power and of love and of a sound mind." Fear is a very real thing, but it's something you were created to overcome.

THE MAJOR MONEY FEARS

One of the best parts of my job is traveling and speaking to people all over the country. The funny thing is, no matter where I go I see people struggling with the same money fears. Over the next two chapters, we're going to look at the top six money fears I see and how to face them.

1. If something bad happens, I won't survive financially.
2. Time is running out. There's no way I can do what I've always wanted to do.
3. I can't win with money because I'm not smart enough.
4. I can't succeed because of how the world works.
5. I'll never be able to get ahead because of the really bad money mistakes I've made.
6. I'm scared I'll end up like my parents.

The first two are fears that psychologist and relationship expert Dr. Les Parrott shares at our Money & Marriage events. We'll look at those two in this chapter, along with practical ways to face them, and we'll look at the last four fears in the next chapter.

FEAR #1: NOT HAVING ENOUGH
"If something bad happens, I won't survive financially."

What if your boss called you in tomorrow morning and told you they were going to have to let you go? What if your child gets sick and you end up with a stack of hefty medical bills? What if your air conditioning breaks in the middle of July and you have to fork over thousands of dollars for a new one? What if there's another global pandemic and the economy shuts down for months? What if . . . ? It's a scary question.

If you're scared you might not have enough money to survive something unexpected, you're not alone. This is a legitimate fear for a lot of people. In fact, it's probably the biggest fear I see in people when it comes to their money. The hard reality is most people in America aren't in a great spot financially. According to a survey by CareerBuilder, 78 percent of Americans live paycheck to paycheck,[5] and the Federal Reserve reports that only 61 percent of Americans can cover a $400 emergency with cash.[6] The majority of people today really can't handle an unexpected emergency.

Lack of security is also *the* top money fear for most women.[7] For years my dad has joked that women have a security gland men do not. He would say it's attached to a woman's face, and when she starts to feel that security gland flare up, you can read it all over her face. I heard him teach this as a kid and teenager and laughed along with the audience, but now that I'm an adult,

I get it completely. Every woman I know has at some point asked, *Are we going to be okay if something bad happens?*

Now for men, this fear may manifest itself a little bit differently. Men often find security in their jobs and what they can provide for their family. Instead of *Will we be okay?* they may wonder "Am I able to earn enough to provide for the needs of my family?" At its root, this is the same fear: Will we have enough?

This fear can be time-specific too. You might be scared about not having enough for this week's groceries or this month's mortgage—a present fear. Or you might be scared about not having enough money saved for retirement or not being able to pay for your kid's college, or not having the ability to take care of your aging parents—a future fear.

This fear is real for a lot of people because of the culture we live in, but here's the deal: This fear of not having enough can also be completely irrational. It can haunt you even if you *do* have money in the bank. This is my money fear. And even though Winston and I have been following the Baby Steps for a long time now, are debt-free, and are consistently investing and giving, every now and then I still ask, "What if the worst of the worst happens? Will we survive? Will we be okay?" And the truth is, yes, we will be okay because we don't owe anyone anything, and we have money saved in the bank. On paper, it can seem irrational for me to have this money fear, but that's the thing about fear—it's really powerful and it's not always logical.

The Emergency Fund

If financial security is one of your fears, own it and name it. Then focus on the truth. The truth is, emergencies will come up. This is a fact of life. And there's a pretty simple way to address this fear: Have an emergency fund. Having money set aside specifically for emergencies can give you an enormous sense of security. If you're new to Ramsey Solutions, I want to quickly share with you our proven plan for your money called the Baby Steps. (If you've been around a while, stay with me. It never hurts to review the basics before building on them.) The Baby Steps are a clear path to winning with money. They also help address a lot of other things—like your fears! The Baby Steps are:

1. Save $1,000 for your starter emergency fund.
2. Pay off all debt (except the house) using the debt snowball.
3. Save three to six months of expenses in a fully funded emergency fund.
4. Invest 15 percent of your household income in retirement.
5. Save for your children's college fund.
6. Pay off your home early.
7. Build wealth and give.

If you fear you won't have enough to cover an emergency, you want to focus on Baby Steps 1–3. And it's important to focus on them in order. You want to begin by saving a starter emergency fund of $1,000. That $1,000 will cover a lot of unexpected emergencies you'd normally put on a credit card, like a car repair or a medical bill. And I want you to save this up fast! Sell something, work overtime, do a budget, and cut your expenses like crazy—whatever it takes. The point is: Get it as soon as possible. Do not take your time, and do not be half-hearted! Get this $1,000 saved like your life depends on it.

After your $1,000 starter emergency fund is saved, your next step is to get out of debt—everything but your mortgage. List out your debts from smallest to largest and pay them off using the debt snowball method. (We'll talk more about exactly how this works later.) After helping millions of people get out of debt, we've found most people typically accomplish this goal in eighteen to twenty-four months. It may take less time or more time, depending on your situation—but this is a *critical* step in taking control of your money. After all your debt is paid off (except your house), bump up that starter emergency fund to three to six months of expenses. This is what we consider a fully funded emergency fund. If you're single and don't have children, three months of expenses may be enough. If you're self-employed, have an irregular income, or have kids and a mortgage, you may want to save six months of expenses.

Now, stop and take that in for just a second. Imagine having *no* payments, except your house payment, and three to six months of expenses saved in the bank. You've also got a budget, and you're disciplined in your spending. You actually have more money coming *in* every month than going *out*! This puts you in a completely different position financially and emotionally. Think about the peace of mind you have. You can breathe again! You're financially stable and can weather a whole lot of storm in that scenario.

And you suddenly have way more options than you ever thought possible. You can quit a job you hate to take a job you love that pays a little less. You can start saving toward a dream. You can start investing in retirement. *You can actually sleep at night.* The possibilities are wide open when you have a solid financial foundation. Now, does this usually happen overnight? No. You have to work the plan, stay dedicated, and make sacrifices—but it can be done no matter your income!

The Debt Snowball

Let me tell you about Elizabeth. She's a school teacher earning a modest income who had $40,000 of debt. She made regular payments but realized the interest kept building and her debt was actually growing. So Elizabeth decided to work the Baby Steps and set aside that initial $1,000 emergency fund. How did she do it? She picked up extra work as a babysitter. Once she had that starter emergency fund in place, she got excited. She told her friends about her determination to get out of debt. She picked up more odd jobs—a bakery job on the weekends, a dog-walking gig, house-sitting. At one point she had eight jobs! *But she did it.* She paid off that $40,000 of debt using the debt snowball, and now she's working on putting aside three to six months of living expenses. Seriously, this *can* be done!

You may be wondering what the debt snowball method is. Let me tell you—it's the best and fastest way to pay off all your debt, and it's exactly how Elizabeth achieved her goal. Here's how it works:

Step 1: List your debts smallest to largest, regardless of interest rate. Pay minimum payments on everything but the smallest one.

Step 2: Attack the smallest debt with a vengeance—get a second job, sell everything you don't need or use, cut back on all your spending. Do whatever it takes! Once that debt is gone, take that payment (and any extra money you can squeeze out of the budget) and apply it to the second-smallest debt while continuing to make minimum payments on the rest.

Step 3: Once that debt is gone, take its payment, and apply it to the next-smallest debt. The more you pay off, the more your freed-up money grows and gets thrown onto the next debt—like a snowball rolling downhill.

Repeat this method as you plow your way through debt until you're debt-free!

Now, I want to be really clear about this: Money doesn't give you all the peace in the world. It's not the ultimate security. It's not a magic wand that makes all of life's troubles suddenly disappear. But if you've been living paycheck to paycheck and in panic mode 24/7, then getting rid of your debt and having an emergency fund will relieve a mountain of stress from your life. Zig Ziglar used to say, "Money isn't the most important thing in the world, but it's right up there with oxygen." If you want to reduce your stress level and you don't already have an emergency fund, start here. It's a total game changer. To learn more about building an emergency fund and the debt snowball, search rachelcruze.com.

FEAR #2: NOT REALIZING YOUR DREAMS
"Time is running out. There's no way I can do what I've always wanted to do."

This fear is another one that hits home for a lot of people. Is there something significant you've always dreamed of doing that doesn't look like it will ever happen?

Maybe you dreamed of going back to school to pursue that degree and career you have such a passion for, but you're older now and it seems so farfetched.

Maybe you always thought you'd live on a nice piece of land one day. But you look up, and you're still in a neighborhood in the suburbs and can't imagine ever having enough money to make that move.

Maybe as a young couple you dreamed of taking your kids to the beach every year. But now the kids are in high school, and you're barely able to make the car payment each month—let alone afford a beach vacation.

Maybe you always planned on getting back to that hobby you loved when you were younger. But your work schedule and family commitments make it seem impossible.

Maybe you had a dream of being outrageously generous whenever you felt led, but you're living paycheck to paycheck and that extra giving seems like it will never happen.

Maybe you wanted to retire at a young age, and as the years tick by, that dream is slowly slipping away.

The Bible says, "Hope deferred makes the heart sick" (Proverbs 13:12). The fear of not realizing your dreams is dangerous because it can slowly drain the life right out of you. Just the thought that you've lost your chance at your dream can cause sadness and depression to creep in and set up house. When this fear takes root, it can paralyze you from within because you don't see a realistic plan to get you there. It stops you from achieving your dream before you even start.

No Dream Killers Here

We all have expectations when it comes to how we think life will go. We'll be married by a certain age or achieve all our career goals by the time we're thirty. We'll live in this type of home or in that city or have this many kids. Sound familiar? Now raise your hand if your life today looks like you thought it would ten years ago. Hmmm . . . not you either?

You guys, there isn't a single one of us whose life has turned out the way we expected. Part of overcoming the fear that we'll never achieve our dreams is to accept that life won't turn out the way we think it will. And that's not always bad!

In *EntreLeadership*, my dad talks about the fable of the tortoise and the hare. You all know it: A tortoise and a hare decide to race. The hare shoots off fast and quickly gets distracted because it knows it's going to win. The tortoise just keeps plugging away, even when its chances of winning look nonexistent. And despite all the odds, the tortoise ends up winning. Why? He never gives up. If there's anything we've learned in almost thirty years at Ramsey Solutions, it's *be the tortoise!* Slow and steady, step by step, walk or crawl (or run) your race—just don't give up! This isn't a sprint. Fix your eyes on your dream and stick to it even when you hit a detour or others seem to be farther along toward their goals.

Keep in mind, too, that some dreams may be tricky to accomplish because of your stage in life. If you love basketball and dream of having season tickets to your favorite NBA team but you also have three small kids at home, it's going to be difficult to carve out enough time—and money—to commit to going to all those games. Your time is limited. If you love photography and dream of buying gear and starting your own business but you're on Baby Step 2 and paying off debt, you need to wait. Your income is limited. If you dream of traveling and have a destination bucket list but just started your first job and don't have vacation days saved up—you need to be patient and save up your money and time off. Sometimes your season of life slows your progress. When this happens, remember it's *temporary*. Don't give up on your dream—just be realistic about what it will take to get there.

For a lot of people, money (either money problems or a lack of money) is the main speed bump on the path to achieving a dream. This sounds obvious, but it holds so many of us back. The first big step to achieving your dream is to make sure your finances are in order. Again, this is why the Baby Steps are so important. It's going to be really hard to chase after your dreams if you don't have the cash to pursue them. Work the Baby Steps. Do them in the right order. If you're in debt, attack it with the debt snowball in Baby Step 2. When your income isn't going toward paying off your past, you'll suddenly have cash to start working toward your future.

If you're on Baby Steps 1–3, you won't be spending money on your dream *yet*, but you can still nurture it along. Talk about it with the people closest to you. Research different parts of it. Read blogs and books. Meet with people who are already doing what you want to do. Volunteer to help them so you can gain experience, or ask to shadow them so you can see what it's really like. Ask questions. This will not only keep you excited about your dream, but it'll also help you learn things that will motivate you on your journey.

Once you've done your homework, build out a timeline. Determine your goal date and work backward. Ask what has to be true between now and then to make your money goals happen. How much do you need to save between now and your target date to save that $1,000 emergency fund? How much do you need to pay off each month between now and your target date to become debt-free? How much money will your dream cost, and what will you do to bring in extra income? Break these goals into smaller chunks and get moving! You can do this! The key here is to not only prepare for your dream, but also to keep your hope burning while you're doing the hard work of building a solid financial foundation. As long as you keep your hope alive, you'll be able to overcome whatever setbacks you face—no matter how long it takes to achieve your dream.

CHAPTER 6

Your Money Fears, Part 2

The four fears we're going to cover in this chapter are ones I've encountered frequently in talking with people about their money. Remember, no one is immune to money fears—even those who have money. As we look at each one, keep in mind the steps to use when dealing with fear:

1. Name it.
2. Focus on the truth.
3. Reach out for help.

Now, hear my heart for a minute: I know that conquering fear isn't always easy. These steps are tools to help you get clarity, get stronger and get support. There will almost certainly be struggle involved as you dig deep to overcome your fears. But as you work through the steps and gain new insight, that struggle will turn into hope and courage to change the things that are holding you back!

FEAR #3: NOT BEING CAPABLE
"I can't win with money because I'm not smart enough."

This is a fear I've heard for years.

"All those people who are winning with money are smart. They understand the complicated math. They're bankers and investment professionals who went to college for this. Of course they're going to win! But I don't know how money works, so it's not going to happen for me."

"I'm not smart enough."

"I'm terrible at math."

"I can't do it."

There are a lot of people who think personal finance is beyond them. And I get it! Money can be an intimidating subject. You start to hear a few theories and funky terms like wraparound annuities, QSEHRAs, backdoor Roth IRAs, and 457(b)s, and it can feel overwhelming quickly. But just because there are words we can't spell and ideas we don't yet understand doesn't mean we can't win with money!

After Winston and I got married, we met with an investment professional to get a handle on combining our money and investments. I was so nervous about that meeting! And you know what? There were parts I didn't understand! That's right: Even Dave Ramsey's daughter, who grew up around money principles her entire life, didn't understand everything about money. But here's the thing: I refused to walk out of that meeting until I understood where we were and what we were going to do. I asked question after question until I had a grasp of our situation—and the fear I had disappeared.

If you're worried you're not smart enough or don't have what it takes to succeed with money, let me tell you a story my friend Chris Hogan shared with me about a man named Ronald Read. Ronald was a janitor and gas station attendant in Vermont. When he died at age 92, a widower, his family discovered he had a net worth of $8 million.[8] This man didn't have a fancy degree in finance. He never made a lot of money and didn't drive a luxury car. He just understood some simple principles. He lived frugally. He invested in things he understood. He asked a lot of questions, and he was patient for decades as his net worth grew. Those are things *anyone* can do.

You're in Charge

If this is one of your money fears, I have great news for you: Personal finance is personal! It doesn't take an MBA in finance to win with money. It's totally within your control because it's based solely on you. And that's great news because handling your money well is *not* complicated. At Ramsey Solutions, we believe managing money well is 80 percent behavior and only 20 percent head knowledge. That means 80 percent of building wealth is about *you* putting some simple principles into practice. Eighty percent of winning with money is about *your* discipline, *your* consistency, *your* daily choices. *You're* the one controlling where your ship goes.

Now for some, this can be bad news because you have to acknowledge you have a lot of responsibility here. You have to learn to control your behavior. You can't spend money you don't have. You can't avoid doing a budget. You can't just do whatever feels good in the moment. (I'm looking at you, last-minute Target runs, Friday night takeout, and financed cars!) You have to be disciplined and intentional to get to a place where you control your money—not the other way around.

So what about the 20 percent head knowledge? You may already know you don't know enough yet, or you might be like my friend Lacy who grew up thinking she knew about money. Her dad was a financial planner, and they talked occasionally about what she needed to do with her money. But then Lacy got out on her own and spent a decade living paycheck to paycheck without knowing why. If you're not currently making progress with your money, it's a good sign you're missing some important information.

If this is you, go back to the basics—things like: Live on less than you make, buy only what you can afford, and stick to the Baby Steps. Make sure you know the difference between a credit card and debit card; learn how to do a zero-based budget; know when to use a checking account, savings account, and money market account; and talk to an investment professional about how to invest. We've got a ton of free information available on our website ramseysolutions.com, so that's a good place to start! The number one mistake people with this fear make is being too intimidated to ask questions. Listen, you don't have to become a financial expert, but you're going to need to learn the basics. I never want you to believe you're not smart enough to win with money because it's simply not true. You *really can* do this!

FEAR #4: EXTERNAL FORCES
"I can't succeed because of how the world works."

"If so-and-so will just get elected, everything will be fine. My student loans will be forgiven, and I'll finally be able to live my life."

"The wrong person is in the White House."

"Congress just passed the most ridiculous law."

"Corporate greed is everywhere."

"We were told to take out student loans, and now the debt is so overwhelming, and there's no way we'll ever get out from under it."

Have you ever heard someone say those things? Have you ever thought those things? There's this belief in our culture—often among my own generation—that says we won't ever get ahead because of factors in life we can't control.

We start blaming our money problems on other people and things:

- "It's not my fault—no one ever taught me!"
- "The system is rigged. People like me can't ever get ahead."
- "The only thing HR people care about are advanced degrees. I'll never get a fair shot at a job."

The truth is there *are* a lot of things completely out of our control. A lot of things in life happen that we have no say in. But this is equally true: Your circumstances don't define you—how you handle them does. You don't control if a company offers you the job, but you make sure you bring your A game to every interview and send thank-you notes afterward. You don't control if you get laid off from your job, but you can be debt-free and have an emergency fund so you're prepared to weather the storm. You don't control if your spouse of seventeen years walks away from your marriage, but you do decide whether or not to start living again. For every person held back by something out of their control, there is someone in a similar situation who overcame it.

Are there external forces we have to overcome? Yes. Do some people face harder battles than others? For sure. But you choose whether you stay in the fight or give up altogether. No one can do that for you.

Your Beliefs Change Everything

What makes one person rise above enormous money challenges and another give up? Their beliefs. What you believe today decides your future. What you believe about money, yourself, and the world shapes how your life will unfold. Every single day you have the power to make decisions that will move you forward financially or set you back. It's up to you.

Stop waiting for someone or something else to change your life. You're just losing time. Time that could be on your side, getting you out of debt or earning compound interest. If your hopes are set on Washington, DC, to fix your life, you'll be waiting a very, *very* long time. No Democrat or Republican is going to change your life. *You* are the one who's going to change your life. Because even if that perfect politician gets elected, they're not king or queen. There are still checks and balances in our political system—which reminds me of the phrase, "It will take an act of Congress."

Ramsey Solutions conducted a study of over ten thousand millionaires, and one of the most fascinating statistics to me was that 97 percent of millionaires believed they could become millionaires.[9] It was within their control. They believed *they* held the key to their success. Part of the secret for most of those ten thousand millionaires was that they believed it was possible. And by the way, 84 percent of them were first-generation millionaires![10] They didn't inherit their wealth; they built it through hard work. Your beliefs matter!

Henry Ford said, "Whether you believe you can do a thing or not, you are right." Ask yourself right now if you believe you have everything you need to get in control, win with money, and be outrageously generous. You don't need to know *how* you're going to accomplish it. Right now, you only have to believe you can. Let me give you an example of how your beliefs can impact your life.

Hailey had been a graphic designer for ten years. She was interested in taking a continuing education class but never had enough money or time off from work when the class was offered. As the years passed, she grew more and more frustrated at her lack of progress. So she finally made the decision to take the next class no matter what. She didn't know how she would arrange the time off or pay for it, but for the first time she believed she could make it happen. And she had six months to figure out how.

Hailey kept working hard at her day job, and a few weeks later, an acquaintance unexpectedly contacted her about designing a logo and website for her small business. The project paid enough to cover the cost of her tuition. When she approached her boss about taking time off for the class, he was delighted she was investing in herself professionally. Since she was paying for the class, he told her she could use flex time instead of vacation days. What made the difference for Hailey? The only thing that changed was her belief that she could do it.

You guys, we have to start here. We have to start believing we can take control of our money and actually win! If we believe the problem is too big for us to solve, *it will be.* If we believe we can conquer the mountain, *we will.* And how we're going to do it will come to us in time.

In addition to controling what you believe, if you focus your energies on the following things, you'll move forward in life.

First, you can control your *work ethic*. Are you willing to work several jobs? Are you hungry enough to learn a new skill so you can get a different job? Are you willing to sell some of your stuff to pay off debt? Hailey was willing to take on extra work to earn her tuition money. Any goal worth achieving is going to require that you work hard.

Second, you can control your *money*. Luke 16:10 says, "Whoever can be trusted with very little can also be trusted with much." Have you made a plan for your money (aka a monthly budget)? Are you saving up for purchases instead of financing them? When Hailey made the extra money, she didn't blow it on stuff she'd seen on her Instagram feed. She also didn't have to play catch-up on her bills because she was already current. She could use that money for the class because she'd been disciplined in her everyday finances.

Third, you can control the *people you hang around*. Be careful who your friends are. The Bible says, "Whoever walks with the wise becomes wise, but the companion of fools will suffer harm" (Proverbs 13:20 ESV). You become more like the people you spend time with. You adopt their mindset, behaviors, and habits. If you hang around with people who have a victim mentality, you start to adopt that type of thinking. If you spend time with people who are committed to achieving their goals, you'll begin to be more productive too. The people you're around most are going to influence you—so choose them wisely.

Make the decision today to win with money. I want you to be so fired up to win that nothing and no one can stand in your way. Then, focus on controlling the things you can. Those are the habits that will help you pay off debt and build wealth so you can live life on *your* terms.

FEAR #5: PAST MISTAKES
"I'll never be able to get ahead because of the really bad money mistakes I've made."

Like we talked about in chapter 1, dealing with your past is a big part of succeeding with money. And the past can *hurt*. It can hurt so bad for so long that it brings down marriages and families. A couple with three children came by our headquarters in 2018 feeling defeated. They were facing $700,000 of past mistakes, all related to failed farming businesses.[11] Their marriage was on rocky ground, and they were exhausted from the stress of it all. Their situation actually sounded a lot like what my parents faced during their bankruptcy. They were looking at some really rough years ahead to clean up the mess, but they were taking responsibility for it and facing it head on. The weight of past mistakes can make you want to give up. It can look too big, too hard, and too scary to even get started—but we have to face our past in order to move forward.

Your Past Doesn't Have to Hold You Back

Like a lot of people, I'm a huge Disney fan. I mean, how can you deny the magic? And nothing says superfan like taking life lessons from animated characters. One of the best Disney movies out there is *The Lion King*. There's this scene toward the end of the film when Simba reunites with the wise monkey Rafiki. Simba sees a message in the clouds from his deceased father reminding him who he is. Then Simba and Rafiki have this exchange:

Simba: "Looks like the winds are changing."
Rafiki: "Ah yes, change is good."

Simba: "Yeah, but it's not easy. I know what I have to do. But going back means I'll have to face my past. I have been running from it for so long."

[*Out of nowhere, Rafiki hits Simba over the head with a stick.*]

Simba: "Ouch, geez, what was that for?"

Rafiki: "It doesn't matter—it is in the past."

Simba: "Yeah, but it still hurts."

Rafiki: "Oh yes, the past can hurt. But the way I see it, you can either run from it or learn from it."

Most people today have to clean up their money mistakes in order to move forward. Lying to your spouse about your finances is a mistake that will take time to heal. Not taking responsibility for your choices is a mistake you won't overcome until you acknowledge that the problem is the person in the mirror. Debt is a mistake that keeps you paying for your past: food you've already eaten, vacations you've already taken, clothes you've already worn (and maybe already gotten rid of!), a degree you earned five years ago. You're going to have to dig out one debt at a time. No one is denying that past mistakes hurt. No one is denying there are consequences we have to face. But let's take Rafiki's advice and learn from the past instead of running from it or ignoring it.

A lot of times the fear of past mistakes takes root because we've confused two very different things. There's a big difference between "I've failed" and "I'm a failure." One is the result of a poor decision; the other is a defining characteristic of who we are. If you're facing the fear of past mistakes, you've got to remember that mistakes are part of being human. We *all* make mistakes. It's not who you are—it's what happened. What matters is what you do now.

If you've made a major money mistake, it's not uncommon to feel guilt or shame. Guilt can be helpful. It can move us to make a better decision next time. But shame is debilitating. Bestselling author Brené Brown defines *shame* as "the intensely painful feeling or experience of believing that we are flawed, and therefore, unworthy of love and belonging."[12] In *The Lion King*, Simba ran away from his life because he thought *he* was a failure. He thought *he* was unworthy. Remember what happened just before Simba faced his past? Don't miss this: Simba gets a message from his father *reminding him who he is*. The order here is everything. Simba had to remember who he really was in order to take on his past mistakes and move forward.

If you think your past is too big to overcome, allow me to help you remember who *you* are. You were not born a failure. You were not born to just get by. You were not born to sleepwalk through life. Who are you?

You are loved.
You are strong.
You can do hard things.
You're here for a reason.

Jeremiah 29:11 says, "'For I know the plans I have for you,' declares the Lord, 'plans to prosper you and not to harm you, plans to give you hope and a future.'" Your life isn't an accident. You matter—and your life matters. Don't brush past this. You've got to start here and gather your courage to face whatever mountain you need to climb, for however long it takes to climb it.

As you face your mistakes, keep in mind your past is a factor in how quickly you get some wins under your belt. Five thousand dollars of debt won't take you as long to pay off as $200,000. Both are possible, but that $200,000 will take longer. One of my friends was telling me about her brother who has $100,000 of student loan debt. The worst part is, he never graduated. So he's walking around with all this debt, no degree, and no job. His stress level and anxiety are so high that he's spiraled downward into depression. But even his situation isn't hopeless. It will be difficult. It will take time and hard work to overcome. But it's a reality he *can* face.

Facing reality is so critical because we all have to handle money every day. This isn't something we can opt out of. You have to choose: Either you're going to continue avoiding your mess and allow it to keep growing like a cavity that turns into a root canal, or you're going to learn from your mistakes, clean up your mess, and move forward. The only real failure is not getting up and going after it again when you fall. You can't avoid the future, but you *can* avoid letting your past control your future.

FEAR #6: REPEATING THE PAST
"I'm scared I'll end up like my parents."

Parents are our first role models. Growing up, we learned things from their example without even realizing it. And then, at some point, we discover that what we thought was normal and the only way to do something, really isn't—like how there are other ways to make spaghetti. And there are other ways to handle money too. Taking on debt, for example, doesn't have to be a way of life. But breaking the habits and patterns of our role models isn't a cakewalk, and there can be a lot of fear around ending up like our parents. This fear can look a lot of different ways.

Sometimes you fear repeating the past because you've watched your parents struggle with money your whole life. You don't actually know that managing money well is possible because you've never seen it done. Or maybe you thought your parents were doing fine, but during a Milestone Moment you realized they weren't. Maybe they didn't have a high-paying job, or maybe they couldn't keep a job. Maybe they have nothing saved for retirement. You look at their situation and fear begins to rise up within you. You think to yourself, *I don't want my life to look like theirs.*

And then there are parents who have so little money that they're forced to move in with their adult children because they literally can't take care of themselves financially. Watching this play out can be incredibly hard. Relationally, it's hard because you love your parents and want to honor them. And it can be just as hard financially because most people barely have enough money to take care of themselves, let alone their parents. This happened to one of my good friends, and I remember her saying, "No matter what, I'm not going to do this to my kids. I'm going to make sure we're smart now so we don't put this burden on our children."

There are also people who grew up in poverty who have a strong fear of ending up back there. I love listening to on-air radio personality and bestselling author Bobby Bones in the mornings. Now, he's done extremely well for himself. If you've listened to him for long, you know he grew up with very little money and has a "deep-rooted fear of being poor again one day." Today he's conservative with money. For a long time he overpaid his monthly utility bills to create a little padding in case he couldn't pay one month.[13] So, if the electric bill came in at $212, he paid $220 just to make sure it was taken care of. He said one morning on his show, "I will never be late on my bills or have someone call me and tell me I owe them money." Overpaying his bills was completely unnecessary (and he doesn't do it anymore), but it was his way of coping with the fear that his utilities would be shut off.

Fear of repeating the past isn't always about having enough money. For some of you, your story isn't that your parents didn't have enough—it's that they had too much. All you saw growing up was excess. It was all about appearances and bigger and better, and now you have zero interest in money or the things it can buy. You already know stuff doesn't make you happy. But if you grew up feeling your parents were superficial and preoccupied with money, you may actually despise or fear wealth.

On the opposite end of the spectrum were parents who made it feel like spending money was a deadly sin. Every single penny was squeezed out—maybe out of necessity, maybe out of fear. My friend Tracy's mom would negotiate the price of everything. And by everything, I mean *everything*. Anytime there was a transaction, she was wheeling and dealing—grocery stores, thrift stores, clothing stores. Even on the rare occasion when she ordered pizza, she would talk the guy into throwing in a free side dish and two-liter bottle of Coke. Tracy spent much of her childhood deeply embarrassed by her mother's behavior because it felt like her mom used people to get stuff.

Who You Serve Is Up to You

If you resonated with any of this, here's what I want you to remember: It's okay to acknowledge that your parents' view of money was unhealthy. And it's okay if they made choices you don't agree with. Rest in the fact you don't have to make your parents' mistakes. It *is* actually possible to handle money wisely, build wealth, have a healthy view of money, and use it only as a tool.

That's all it is anyway. Having nice things isn't the issue. The issue is with the person in the mirror. Matthew 6:24 says, "No one can serve two masters. Either you will hate the one and love the other, or you will be devoted to the one and despise the other. You cannot serve both God and money." Notice it doesn't say "you can't have money *and* serve God." It says you can't *serve* both. Remember, money is only a tool. It shouldn't be the most important thing in your life.

If you fear repeating the past and ending up like your parents, you need to find new money role models. Maybe it's someone at church, someone in your community, a good friend, or your *Financial Peace University* class leader. Find someone who's actually living out the values you want to live. Ask if they will meet with you and teach you how to do it. If you grew up with people who lived with debt, get to know someone who is debt-free. If you grew up in poverty, get to know someone who grew up in poverty, built wealth, kept it, and gives generously. If you grew up with parents who served money and not God, get to know someone who uses money as a tool to help their family and others. I'm not saying this is an easy process. But there are things you can do to improve your life. You're not doomed to repeat your parents' mistakes. You can learn new information and new behaviors and choose new habits. That's what's really exciting: You have the power to choose for yourself who you will serve.

WHERE FEAR LEADS US

You may have a money fear I didn't specifically call out in this chapter. If you do, face it using the same three steps we've talked about in this chapter: Call it out, focus on the truth, and reach out for help. Fear isn't usually something we deal with once and then it goes away forever. It's something we will experience throughout life. That might initially sound discouraging, but we have to remember that *fear is a gift*. Think about where fear leads us. I was talking with Dr. Chip Dodd, a bestselling author, teacher, and counselor, and he said, "Fear is a feeling God has given us. It's not sin. It can be scary, but fear is just the recognition that we need help." Fear leads us to reach out to God and others to ask for help.

If you look back over this chapter, you can see how each fear is an invitation to ask for help. These fears are circling some of the basic, universal questions we all have as human beings:

- The fear of not having enough is often asking, "Am I safe?"
- The fear of not realizing dreams is often asking, "Does my life have meaning and purpose?"
- The fear of not being capable and being held back by external forces is often asking, "Can I believe in myself?"
- The fear of past mistakes is often asking, "Can I be forgiven?"
- The fear of repeating our parents' mistakes is often asking, "Am I a failure?"

Each of these fears is resolved in healthy relationships with God and other people. *We were never meant to do life alone.*

The way to overcome fear isn't to act tougher. The way to overcome fear is to be vulnerable. The way to overcome fear is to be known. So ask for help! Your church can help. Someone in your community can help. And we can help! Ramsey Solutions exists to help you take control of your money and create a life you love. So don't let fear control you. Embrace it and the gifts it brings to your life.

NOW IT'S YOUR TURN

1. Review the list of money fears below, then identify which you have. Write them down and rank them from biggest to smallest.

   Fear of not having enough—"If something bad happens, we won't survive financially."

   Fear of not realizing your dreams—"Time is running out. There's no way I can do what I've always dreamed of doing."

   Fear of not being capable—"I can't win with money because I'm not smart enough."

   Fear of external forces—"I won't ever get ahead because of how the world works."

   Fear of past mistakes—"I'll never be able to get ahead because of the really bad money mistakes I've made."

   Fear of repeating the past—"I'm scared I'll end up like my parents."

2. For each one, think through the last time you experienced that fear. How did it block your creativity or limit your options?

3. For each fear, write down its opposite truth and spend some time each day this week focusing on what you wrote. Then talk to someone who has that same fear and find out how they handle it and overcome it.

Here's an example:

My major money fear is of external forces. I don't think I'll ever get ahead because the world is stacked against me.

The truth is, I can be in control of my money. I can choose how to budget it, spend it, save it, and invest it. I can also choose to persevere through the tough times and never give up. It's up to me.

4. If you're married, how do you and your spouse need to come together in order to face your fears as a team? Are there any conversations you need to have? If you're single, who can you talk with about your money fears?

CHAPTER 7

How You Respond to Money Mistakes

One of the things I love to do at night to unwind is turn on a TV show. It could be a mindless reality show, the nightly news, or something on Bravo or HGTV. It's funny because cable is a non-negotiable item in our budget. More than once Winston has said to me, "Can't we just be normal millennials and stream everything?" But I just can't. For me, the DVR is a must for the shows I miss, plus it lets me fast-forward through commercials. Cable gives me options.

The other thing I love—and most people cringe at this—is politics. I love the job I have now, obviously. But if there was an alternate universe, I'd be living in Manhattan, working as a political correspondent for a news channel and making frequent trips to Washington, DC, for special reports. (PS: That will never happen, so don't worry, Winston!) I love election season and watch all the coverage. I'm probably the only person in the world who enjoys campaign commercials. I watch every debate, and then stay up into the wee hours of the night watching voting results come in. I find it thrilling.

My friends know about my twin passions for cable and politics, so recently a friend recommended that I watch a documentary on Anthony Weiner, a former congressman from New York who faced a huge scandal. A few years later, he ran for mayor of New York City. My friend said the documentary followed him through his mayoral run and through all the ins and outs of his campaign. This camera crew had insider access throughout the campaign, and during filming mid-campaign, another scandal broke out. This was some terrible stuff, but for some reason, Weiner continued to let the cameras roll. So the documentary shows the scandal breaking in real time and what he, his wife, and his team were doing to try to downplay and fix it. My friend promised this was drama on an epic scale.

So one afternoon while my girls were napping, I decided to find the documentary and watch it. It was available on demand through our cable provider. Renting it cost $19.99—a pretty hefty fee for a rental. But my heart was set on seeing it! I figured we'd pay that much to see it in a theater, and this way, we didn't even need to pay a babysitter. I bit the bullet and mentally put that $19.99 in the "Rachel" line item of our budget. Needless to say, I watched it and it was fantastic! I didn't think much about it again until a few weeks later.

One night I came home from work, and Winston was already there. He was in the kitchen on his phone looking very frustrated. I heard him say, "No. We are not paying for that. You guys do this to us almost every month, adding extra fees or jacking up your prices . . . so, no."

There was a pause, so I whispered to him, "Who are you talking to?"

He looked at me, rolling his eyes. "The cable company," he whispered.

Oh, I knew this conversation well. Winston and the cable company go at it at least three times a year about our bill. He kept shaking his head in frustration and then blurted out, "No! We did not rent a video called *Weiner!*"

Oh, the horror! I looked at Winston with wide eyes and started panicking. I began nodding my head wildly. "Yes! Yes, I did! I rented that! That title sounds awful, but it was about politics! An election!"

Winston paused to take in my unexpected confession and then sheepishly replied to the customer service rep, "I'm sorry. My mistake. My wife actually rented *Weiner.*"

Just hearing him say it out loud was embarrassing and hysterical all at the same time! I started shouting so the person on the other end of the phone could hear: "It's a *documentary* about a former congressman running for mayor of New York City!"

Winston quickly ended the call and started laughing. "Babe, why didn't you tell me?" he asked.

I told him I'd honestly forgotten. Plus—shout out to my free spirits here!—who looks over a cable bill that closely anyway? (I'm so not the detailed one in our marriage.)

As you can imagine, we had a really good laugh about the whole thing.

Why did I share that? Because Winston and I have been managing our money together for over a decade, and we still mess up. Things go wrong. We forget to communicate about a purchase. Life doesn't always work out the way we plan. Thankfully, because we're intentional, when we make mistakes they're usually not that costly, emotionally or otherwise. We're proactive and regularly work together on our money. But life still happens, and it affects our money and relationships.

This is true for all of us. Every single one of us makes mistakes with our money. Some are small, like forgetting to sign a check or misplacing cash or forgetting to pay a bill on time. Some are larger, more expensive mistakes like overspending on Christmas gifts or buying a car you really can't afford. And some happen *to* you—like when someone charges you incorrectly on a bill. Each mistake requires a response, but most people don't stop to think about *how* they respond or how it affects them. Instead, most people respond automatically or because it's what they feel like they should do. And while not all money mistakes will cost you a lot of money, you can pay a tremendous price in your relationships—both with yourself and with others. So in addition to your childhood, reflecting on your childhood money classroom, identifying your unique money tendencies, and overcoming your money fears, it's important that you understand how you respond to money mistakes—because no one is perfect and mistakes are going to happen.

THE GRACE SCALE

Think about the last time you faced a money mistake, whether it was your own mistake or a mistake someone else made that impacted you. How did you react? Did you write it off as something that couldn't be helped? Did you roll your eyes, annoyed by it? Did you obsess over it for days and weeks?

When facing money mistakes, we can sometimes respond either by giving too much grace or by not giving enough grace. When we extend too much grace, forgiveness and compassion flow freely, but the injured party still gets hurt and no one learns a better way. When we extend too little grace, there's tough love and by-the-book living but little heart or humility. So where are you? Keep in mind, depending on the situation, you can flip-flop between sides.

The Grace Scale

| TOO MUCH GRACE | ←——————→ | NOT ENOUGH GRACE |

WHEN YOU GIVE TOO MUCH GRACE

We all like to be the recipient of grace—to have a soft place to land when we fall. Those who respond gracefully are those we love to run to when we've made a mistake. They are generous, kind, and forgiving. There's a lot of empathy and compassion. But it can go too far when we're talking about money.

As we talk about giving too much grace in response to money mistakes, remember we're not talking about too much grace when it comes to *sin*. As a Christian, I can hear some of my fellow brothers and sisters out there saying, "Rachel, there is an endless amount of grace!" And that is true—thank you, Jesus— when we're talking about salvation. But when we're talking about our response to *money mistakes*, it's possible to extend so much grace that we end up hurting the people involved.

So how can too much grace hurt people? I'm going to illustrate this by using the extremes of the grace scale. Obviously, not everyone is going to fall in one of the extremes, but I would encourage you to read these descriptions carefully. The tricky thing is *most people have no idea that how they respond to money mistakes can actually do more harm than good.* So read closely and take an honest look at your behavior. You may discover you're unintentionally hurting the people you love the most.

The extreme of giving too much grace is . . . enabling. I know, it's a hard word to swallow. An *enabler* is someone who "enables another to persist in self-destructive habits by providing excuses or by making it possible to avoid the consequences of such behavior."[14] Enablers extend grace upon grace and chance after chance to the people in their lives. There is no end to their belief that the person they're helping is trying and will do better the next time. They have the best of intentions to really help people and love people well. If you see an overweight dog, you can probably bet its owner is an enabler. They have a hard time saying no even to their pets!

When a bill is paid late and a late fee is tacked on the next month, they say, "Oh, well." And when the late fees start to stack up and they don't have enough money for groceries, out comes the credit card with an easy tug. "It happens!" they say, believing next month will go better. The allowances are unending and there's no course correction for the problem.

Enablers make lots of room for money mistakes, but unfortunately, it's often to their own detriment. They don't usually have boundaries and rarely take a stand. Their great fear is being mean, which makes it easy for others to take advantage of them. They can also feel so badly about something from the past that they overcompensate for it in the present.

It's so important for enablers to recognize when their help has stopped helping and is now harming—and it's often very hard for them to see. But in an enabling situation, more help is like letting an alcoholic have a drink. The enabler is actually encouraging and prolonging the disease. It can be easy to spot an enabling situation between other people, but we need to first address that some of us enable *ourselves*. And when it comes to money, it really comes down to excuses.

Here are some excuses I hear from people trying to justify their mistakes:

- "I overspend because I'm just not good at planning."
- "I ran up my credit card debt because I hate my job and I needed that vacation."
- "I hid another purchase from my husband because I don't want to stress him out."
- "I can't follow your advice on buying a home because I live in California. Real estate prices are just too high."
- "With my schedule, I can't drive for a delivery service in the evenings, so a part-time job just doesn't work for me."
- "I'm so stressed out that there's no way I can cook dinner tonight. I don't care that it's not in my budget—I'm getting takeout on the way home."

Listen, none of these excuses make mistakes go away. Nor do they excuse the bad behaviors. I'm not going to be mean to you if you're making excuses, but saying "Oh, it's okay! Mistakes happen!" over and over in these circumstances isn't going to help you or your budget. Excusing bad behavior will stop you dead in your tracks from building wealth and living the life you want.

If any of this sounds familiar, there's probably a reason why. If you've been giving yourself too much grace, I want you to hear me say that *no one here is the exception to the rule*. Not me and not you. If you want to win with money, you have to manage it wisely. The longer you enable your own bad behaviors, the bigger your financial mess will be and the longer it will take to clean up. So stop giving yourself a get-out-of-jail-free card. Even if you get a big financial break at some point, if you haven't already learned wise money habits, you'll blow through that big break only to keep repeating the past. So either way, it's in your best interest to face your behavior head on. It's time to face your mess, friend. You won't be alone. We've got a *huge* community of people who will support you and cheer you along, and we have a ton of resources that will coach you—but you've got to do the work. No one else can do it for you.

ENABLING OTHERS

"He's really *trying*."

A sweet lady said this to me about her son. Her son lived with her, and she supported him financially. That situation in and of itself isn't always bad. But then she went into more detail and red flags started flying. Her son wasn't a 4-year-old kid;

he was a 34-year-old man who dropped out of school a decade before. He'd been living with her ever since, unable to hold down a job. This grown man should have been living an independent financial life but was using his mother's bank account as his personal ATM.

My heart broke as this woman shared her distress. She couldn't see the real issue. She didn't realize *she* was the problem. She'd extended way too much grace. She'd never allowed her son to experience full independence and be accountable for his own decisions, financial or otherwise. While physically he was a grown man, really, he was a little boy whose mom always cleaned up the mess he left behind. He'd never felt the pain of his choices or learned a better way.

As a mom, I totally understand the struggle this woman felt! The love you have for your child is unlike any other relationship in your life. They literally depend on you for their life! Especially us mama bears out there—we want to protect our children no matter their age. But think about it from a different perspective. Pediatrician and author Dr. Meg Meeker said:

We're setting our kids up for failure when we teach them that what they really need is more of us and less of themselves. A great parent finds ways to allow children to fail so that they can teach that child one of the most important lessons in life: "You can fail, but Mom and Dad will never stop loving you. We'll show you how to stand back up on your feet and try again." If you really want to teach a child how to succeed, you have to teach them how to plow through failure.[15]

Meeker wrote this for a parent of a young child, but man, I think it applies to parents of grown children too. We all need to make mistakes and experience consequences so we can grow into resourceful, mature adults. When we enable another person, we short-circuit their learning curve and end up hurting them.

Enabling doesn't stop with parents and kids either. It can happen between anyone, including extended family and friends. It's really easy to see a need and want to help, but suddenly, you look up and realize you've been helping for far too long. My friend Lauren told me she'd had a friend, a single guy in her friend group, who was struggling financially. He lost his job and couldn't pay his rent one month, so she covered it for him. The next month, the same thing happened again. She was genuinely happy to do it for him while he got back on his feet. Then, in month three of paying his rent, a mutual friend shared with her that this same guy had asked her for help too. The helping turned unhealthy because the struggling guy wasn't learning how to help himself. He was blowing the extra cash on stuff he didn't need. So be on the lookout for these types of situations. Extending grace when it comes to money mistakes is good, but extending it too far causes damage.

When it comes to where I fall on the grace scale, I'm definitely on this side. I usually assume everyone is trying their best, and I can be flexible and go with the twists and turns of life. I don't get freaked out when rules are broken or people make mistakes. I assume they will learn from what happened and move on and not make that mistake again. As I've gotten older though, I tend to get impatient with people when the same mistake is made over and over again. So over the years, I've moved closer to the middle of the scale, but I still can give too much grace when something goes wrong.

THIRD-PARTY ENABLERS

There's one other category of enabling we need to talk about before moving on: when someone you love is an enabler. This happens to a lot of people, and it can be really tricky to navigate. Maybe your parents are enabling your adult sibling. Or your sibling could be enabling their own child. It's so dang hard to watch someone you love being taken advantage of. And a lot of times your loved one doesn't even realize it's happening.

I have a friend whose mom has been bailing out her son (my friend's half brother) for years. Because her mom divorced her first husband when she was fairly young, she'd spent years feeling guilty about how it affected her son. So now my friend's brother is in his midforties and keeps asking their mom—who doesn't have a lot of money—for more and more help. It's been going on for years, and my sweet friend is understandably upset at her brother. But what I wanted her to realize is that it's not all her brother's fault. *The fault is also her mom's.* That can actually be a pretty tough realization to have. So what is she to do?

Offering advice on this topic is tricky because these situations are complex. So many factors come into play. There are times when it's completely inappropriate for you to say anything at all. And there are other times when your guidance and direction as an outsider can bring truly helpful insight. But before you go speaking your mind, you need to be really clear on one thing: *You cannot change other people.* Let that sink in for a moment. As much as that might frustrate you, other people's behavior is not your responsibility. You do not and *should not* have control over other people's lives. That's out of your hands. This may feel maddening at first, but it's actually really freeing.

Once you're really clear that you can't change anyone, you realize all you can do is offer some feedback. If you're absolutely determined to speak your mind with the lovable enabler in your life, remind yourself to create reasonable expectations for the outcome. The old saying is true: You can lead a horse to water, but you can't make him drink. Just because you offer some truth doesn't mean the situation will change. It might, but it might not. And if it doesn't, take heart: It's not your problem to solve. So let yourself off the hook. Double down on your own efforts to win with money and determine to be a good example. Pray for them. And if you're holding on to anger or fear about the situation, focus on working through that and letting it go. If you don't know how, seek the help of a professional counselor. It's totally possible for you to win with money personally and live free of anger and fear over how other people are handling their money.

Whether you're enabling yourself or someone else, you have the power to stop making excuses and take steps to find balance on the grace scale. Let's look at those steps.

FIRST STEPS TO FINDING BALANCE

If you've extended too much grace to yourself or someone else when it comes to money mistakes, *the first step is to recognize it's an issue*. This is probably the hardest step. When you're neck-deep into enabling, it's hard to recognize that *your* actions are the problem. You have to own this. If you don't know if you're enabling yourself or someone else, ask the trustworthy people around you. Someone has probably already told you the truth. If no one has said anything, ask a trusted friend who will tell you the truth. Now, don't go asking your sister who's still enabling her own daughter. Find someone with a solid track record of living wisely. Once you know you're enabling someone, then you have to decide to do something different.

If you're in an enabling situation, *the second step is to set a boundary and stick to it.* If you've been giving money to a family member for far too long or your adult child has moved back in with you and there's no hope in sight that they're moving out, you need to determine and communicate boundaries. Set limits on what you're willing to do. Set a time limit on the duration of your help and what you expect in return. And be clear about what will happen if those expectations aren't met. The conversation may be awkward and difficult, but it's absolutely necessary—not just for your own sanity, *but for the good of the other person.* You want to give them the dignity of standing on their own two feet, and you can't do that if you're a constant safety net.

If you've been enabling yourself, write down the mistake you keep making and what triggers you to make that mistake. Then create a plan for what you'll do differently when that trigger happens again. For example, if you're triggered to shop online after a hard day, find a friend you can call to get coffee with instead. Then choose someone to hold you accountable to the new behavior.

We'll walk through more specifics of healthy boundaries in chapter 9. For now I want to remind you that we're talking about extreme cases here. If your son or daughter just graduated and needs to move back in for three months before their apartment lease begins, I'm all for it. You've got some natural boundaries in place in that scenario, and it's not a chronic problem. Change will be necessary, though, when you're enabling bad and ongoing financial behaviors.

WHEN YOU DON'T EXTEND ENOUGH GRACE

On the opposite side of the grace scale are those who respond to money mistakes without enough grace. Again, for simplicity, I'm going to talk about this side of the scale using its extreme. In this case, the extreme of withholding grace is *legalism*. If enablers are the rule breakers, the legalists are the rule keepers. They *love* the rules. For them it's all about right and wrong and black and white.

The other day a friend of mine ordered lunch at a drive-through restaurant for her big family. When she got home, she unpacked the order and realized they'd shorted her four side items. She combed through the receipt, and sure enough, she'd paid for every item she'd ordered, including those missing sides. My friend got so upset. She was mad at herself for not checking the order before she drove off and mad at the restaurant for making a mistake in the first place. Her family didn't mind—they were happy with what she brought home—but my friend couldn't eat. Instead, after she poured over the receipt, she called the restaurant to complain, then drove back to collect her eight-dollar refund. She was anything but happy as she waited for the manager to fix the mistake.

The next day, as she thought through the incident, she had to shake her head at herself. She had totally overreacted and she knew it. Had a money mistake happened? Yes. Was it costly? Financially, not really—but she hurt herself by getting so upset about the situation. Would it have been better to offer grace in this circumstance? For sure. And experience tells me she might have gotten both her refund *and* a free meal out of it if she'd been more gracious.

When you tend toward withholding grace, you care deeply about integrity and doing things right. This is admirable and important, but legalists can take these things too far. They end up sacrificing people and relationships in their pursuit of being right. In the drive-through mishap, my friend was way too hard on herself and way too hard on the teenagers scrambling to put together her order during the dinner rush. Legalists can sometimes forget that efficiency isn't our highest good—love is.

Now clearly, we need principles and rules. Without them our world would be anarchy. But being principled is not the same thing as being legalistic. You can have very strong principles without being legalistic. For example, I believe wholeheartedly in the Baby Steps. Winston and I live them every day. That's being principled. Legalism is being unwilling to show compassion for a mistake or misunderstanding. It creeps in when there are rules without any love, discussion, or understanding.

If you lean toward the legalist side of the scale, it's hard to extend grace because being right feels more important to you than being in relationship, even with yourself. A counselor I know once said, "You can be right, or you can be married." It's the same idea here. You can take principles so seriously that you can't let yourself (or others) off the hook because you "know better." Believing strongly in principles doesn't make you a legalist. But favoring rightness over relationships, obedience over love, and rigidness over compassion does.

One of the heartbreaking things about refusing grace is that it causes people to be really, really hard on themselves. I have some dear friends who put themselves on this side of the scale, and they talk regularly about how brutally harsh their inner critic is. If they fail to live up to their impossibly high standards—which is going to happen—their world comes crashing down and their inner critic goes into hyperdrive. When they make a money mistake, they beat themselves up again and again, thinking, *I am so stupid. Why did I do that?*

That's why it's important that we stop and say this again: *Nobody is perfect.* Not even you. Money mistakes will happen. You will not get it right 100 percent of the time. It simply cannot be done. If you're a legalist when it comes to money mistakes, this is so important for you to fully take in. You need to understand it both in your head and your heart. It will be a long, hard life if you keep replaying your mistakes.

We're all going to fail—but that doesn't mean we're failures. Like we talked about in chapter 6, that's a huge difference. Every one of us can say, "I failed." But "I'm a failure" is a lie meant to stop us in our tracks. If you understand that mistakes will happen, that they don't make you bad or a failure, you respond differently to them. You see them for what they are, and you get back up, dust yourself off, and try again.

LEGALISM TOWARD OTHERS

I remember a lady coming up to me after one of my events, and she looked so sad. She began to tell me how her husband had committed financial infidelity. He'd hidden purchases from her, and she'd just found out the night before. My heart began to break for this woman.

I began to imagine late payment notices and bankruptcy proceedings, and well, I kind of went to the worst-case scenario. When situations like this happen, the unsuspecting spouse feels deeply betrayed. Trust is broken. Communication breaks down even more. It's such a hard situation! So I had a lot of compassion for her.

I asked a few follow-up questions to help me give her guidance, and she told me, "Yes, he went to Chick-fil-A three times last week and didn't tell me."

I looked at her like, *You have got to be kidding me.* Number one: It's Jesus chicken. And number two: He probably forgot! His whopping total was probably $25, and she was talking like she was about to separate from the poor guy.

Those who have legalistic tendencies are as hard on others as they are on themselves, and they often have a hard time gaining perspective. If a rule is broken, it's *broken*—whether it's $25 or $25,000. Again, the intention is admirable. I have a lot of respect for this because integrity and doing the right thing are for sure important. If this is you, though, I need you to hear something: Living with you can be tough.

If you've ever been close to someone who's legalistic, you have some idea of how exhausting it can be. You feel like you'll never measure up, no matter how hard you work to earn their approval. It's like the bar to keep them happy is always just a few inches out of reach. The crushing reality is that legalists can end up breaking the spirit of those they love the most.

Those who lean toward legalism tend to give love conditionally. For these people, love and affection are given only in return for good behavior if the other person is performing their duties properly. If someone doesn't measure up to their impossible standards, they can disengage and remove their affection. This mentality is fundamentally flawed because literally no one is perfect. I once heard a young man in his early twenties say, "If someone hurts me, I cut them out of my life. No exceptions." This guy had obviously been hurt deeply in the past, but if he follows through with that statement, he will be alone for the rest of his life. None of us can live up to his standard—not even him.

Another area where legalists can struggle is with judging others. They often make snap decisions without knowing the full story. A lot of enthusiastic Ramsey Solutions fans can probably relate to this. If you see someone driving a new car, you may automatically think, *Oh, I bet they took out a loan for that car. What a shame.* Or you see a friend posting beautiful pictures on social media from their European vacation and your next thought is, *That's extravagant. They probably put all of that on a credit card!* But you don't know the details of that person's life. When I was a teenager and judging other people's actions, my parents would tell me: "Rachel, you have a full-time job taking care of yourself. Quit worrying about what other people are doing." The truth is, even if you're right, even if someone used debt to make those purchases, it's not your job to worry about it—because it's none of your business!

MOVING TOWARD GRACE

You may immediately know if you struggle with not extending enough grace for money mistakes. But if you're not sure, ask someone you trust what they've seen in your life. Doing this can make you feel vulnerable—and you have to be okay getting honest feedback—but it will be incredibly helpful to learn how others perceive you.

Also, when you get that feedback, I encourage you to spend some time reflecting on what causes you to respond that way. As a person of faith, when I go to this extreme, those are the areas and the times when I've stopped trusting God. In those times, I've put too much pressure on myself to fix (or control) a situation. Reflecting on where you are on this scale can help you see the difference between what is *yours* to control and what is *God's* to control.

Then, when money mistakes happen—especially minor ones —remind yourself it's going to be okay. Living with a super black-and-white perspective is not good for anybody. It's too limiting. It limits your relationships, and it limits the grace you give yourself and others. What's critical is that you learn to move on and not let money mistakes define you or your relationships. Learning to relax a little will bring more lightheartedness and even happiness into your life.

If you lean toward legalism, practice giving grace even when you don't think the person deserves it. There are lots of ways to do this. Choose a relationship in your life where you've been strict and back off, allowing room for mistakes. If you're married, you'll probably want to choose your spouse. Usually one spouse (ahem, nerds) is all about the budget and the money rules—period. But if your free spirit spouse makes a mistake here or there, instead of harping on it, just say the simple words, "It's okay. There's grace for that." Then let go of any offense you feel. If the mistake keeps happening, have a conversation about it, but just offering forgiveness for the mistake is a great place to start.

Another way to practice extending grace is to ask yourself if what just happened is going to matter in five years. If my child takes a Sharpie to my brand-new chair, I may be sad or frustrated—but it's just a chair. Your spouse overspending on groceries the first few months you're learning to budget isn't the end of the world. Forgetting to pay a bill on time isn't ideal, but you won't remember it happening in five years. Even bigger mistakes, like buying a car you can't afford, can be overcome in less than five years. So practice extending grace and letting go of past mistakes. Living in a grace-filled, forgiving environment leads to a far more enjoyable life.

Now that we've explored what it looks like to respond to money mistakes with too much grace and not enough grace, I want us to talk about how to find a healthy balance between the two.

CHAPTER 8

The Best Way to Respond When Money Mistakes Happen

As a mom, I get a feeling in my stomach when my kids are in the next room over and I hear something crash to the floor. This happens a lot at our house because our kids are young right now. When it happens, I literally feel it in my gut because I know in the next moment I'll need to spring into action. I'll rush into the next room to find a crying child who's scared and needs to be comforted. There will probably be a mess to sweep up and hurt feelings to soothe.

In such moments, I know I need to extend grace out of love. Because whether you're a kid or an adult, a mistake is painful, and we all need the acceptance and compassion of grace. But at the same time, I often need to make mistakes a teachable moment, like when I'm reminding my child not to climb on the counter as I'm reaching for an ice pack to place on a bruised knee. This can be a hard balance to strike.

There was a story a while back about a couple in their forties who were drowning in debt. They had a healthy income (over $150,000) but had no savings and hundreds of thousands of dollars of debt.[16] What came in each month went right back out in monthly payments, and they hadn't even *started* paying off her student loans. They shopped at thrift stores because it's all they could afford unless they put it on one of their eleven credit cards, which is exactly what they did to get a tuxedo for their son's prom night. And when their dog got sick, they didn't have the cash to put her down, so that went on a credit card too. (Imagine getting that bill in the mail the next month. *Heartbreaking!*)

What's interesting here is that the wife's parents had actually bailed them out once already. Even though her parents were of modest means, they dipped into their retirement savings and gave the couple a huge amount of money to pay off creditors so they were debt-free except for their student loans. They showed their daughter and son-in-law a ton of acceptance and compassion. But what happened? There wasn't any course correction mixed in with all that grace. The couple didn't learn from their mistakes nor did they change their behavior. And so they promptly dug themselves right back into the same pit again—but this time it's even worse. They're so embarrassed by what's happened they've kept it a secret from her parents. Just imagine what it's like for them to attend family gatherings now, carrying the weight of that guilt and shame.

I'm sure her parents believed they were doing something really good for their daughter by paying off that debt. But the heartbreaking reality is that they did nothing more than flush part of their retirement down the drain. It did nothing to help this couple long term.

GRACE AND TRUTH

What's interesting about the grace scale is that it points us to the two things that will keep us centered when we face money mistakes: Enabling points to *grace* and legalism points to *truth*. We need both of them to respond well to money mistakes.

When we're in the heat of the moment facing a mistake, we often struggle to know exactly how much grace to offer and how much correction to give. A simple benchmark to remember is the Golden Rule. Now, before you go rolling your eyes, just try putting yourself in the other person's shoes and think for a minute about how you would want to be treated.

A while back Winston and I saved up for and bought a new car—a minivan. I drove it home from the dealership that night, so excited about how much easier it would make transporting our family of five. The very next day I loaded up my oldest to take her to preschool. I got in my new car, so pumped to drive it, and as I was pulling out of the garage I heard a crunch. My stomach dropped. I braked immediately and may have said a choice word or two, praying my daughter didn't hear me! I dreaded getting out of the car to see the damage.

Apparently the garage door wasn't open all the way, and the top of the van hit the bottom of the door. You know those little fin-looking things on top of cars toward the back of the roof? Well, I learned those aren't just for decoration—who knew they have a satellite, GPS technology, and radio antennas inside? Apparently, the bottom of the garage door sliced that little fin right off and took some of the roof of the van with it. And all those little computer chips were all over our garage floor. I mean it was *not good*, and we had only had this van for *one day*! I couldn't believe it. Out of all the years of me pulling in and out of a garage, why now? Why this day?

Winston was at work, and I had to tell him. I was dreading it, because I was mad at myself. Plus, the car was only one day old! And let's be honest, this would never have happened to Winston. He's methodical and takes his time. I, on the other hand, am like a race car driver pulling out of the garage! I knew he was in a meeting, so I texted and said, "Um, I may have broken the van."

He texted back and asked if anyone was hurt.

"No, thankfully," I said, "if you don't count the little fin on top of the van as a person—because that thing was demolished."

He texted back: "It's fine! We'll just have to get it fixed."

I asked him later that night why he wasn't more frustrated by what I did and he said, "Well, we all make mistakes, and if it were me, that's how I would want you to react."

If you're the husband who went to Chick-fil-A three times one week and forgot to tell your wife, how would you want to be treated? Like a criminal or with understanding? If you're the adult son who's still living at home with mom supporting you, what's in your best interest? Remaining dependent on your mom as an adult? Or learning how to stand on your own two feet and manage your money and life? Thinking through how you would want to be treated is a really good litmus test to help you decide how to respond to money mistakes.

GRACE AND TRUTH LEAD TO
GOOD BOUNDARIES

We've talked about the differences between enabling and legalism, but interestingly, they have one striking similarity: They're both evidence of a lack of boundaries. On one of his visits to *The Dave Ramsey Show*, Dr. Henry Cloud said boundaries are like property lines around your home, telling you where you end and someone else begins.[17] They tell you what you do and don't control. Violating boundaries—invading someone else's territory—only leads to hurting others. Do you want someone else invading your territory? But that's exactly what both enabling and legalistic behaviors do.

Even the most amateur gardener knows that what you plant is what will grow. Your actions today directly affect your future. If you plant peanuts, you'll get peanuts. If you plant poor choices, you'll reap poor consequences. But if you keep going into someone else's garden and digging up their poor consequences (enabling), they never get the opportunity to learn from their mistakes. Or if, because of your controlling nature, you tell them where to put the garden, what to plant, when to plant it, and how to prune each and every stem (legalism), they never learn how to make decisions for themselves. Either way, you're stopping the other person from developing into a mature adult by eliminating their ability to learn from their mistakes.

We too often label mistakes as bad when, really, *mistakes are our teacher*. Mistakes offer us accurate feedback in real time. They teach us how to think critically and how to solve problems. They make us better. We have to get comfortable with failure, our own and others', because it's how we learn a better way. Our challenge when a money mistake happens is not to beat ourselves—or someone else—up but to be curious about the mistake. What is it teaching you? What led you to making that choice? What conversations do you need to have? Is there anything you need to *stop* doing? Is there anything you need to *start* doing? When you respond to money mistakes with both grace and truth, you understand how valuable mistakes are for everyone.

WHAT HEALTHY BOUNDARIES LOOK LIKE

Grace and truth lead to healthy boundaries, and healthy boundaries lead to healthy relationships and a rich life. So what does this look like in real time? A person who does grace and truth well is willing to help but isn't controlled by the outcome. Other people's mistakes don't turn their world upside down. They recognize and are good with the fact that they can only control themselves, their thoughts, and actions. It's not their job to fix anyone else or bail them out. They also tend to be people with a lot of humility, a lot of peace, and a lot of wisdom.

Here's an example of what grace and truth look like using a situation I get asked about a lot: when someone you love is asking you for money. Keep in mind the principles in this example will remain the same no matter who the other person is. Here's the scenario: You're married and in your thirties. You and your spouse both work, and you have two young children. Your mom recently confided in you that she and your dad—both in their late fifties—are facing significant financial distress. Your mom has been a teacher for many years and is close to retirement, but your dad was laid off eighteen months ago. He's been looking for work all this time but hasn't found anything. Because they have so much debt, they've now run out of savings and are behind on several key bills, including their mortgage. She's tearful as she tells you what's going on, and you're absolutely crushed by her words. You knew it had been tough but assumed all along they were in decent financial shape. Now she's asking for help so they don't lose the house. What do you do?

First, take a deep breath. Realizing your parents are underwater financially can rock your world because you've believed something different up until this point. Then, like we've talked about, make sure you know that their money mistakes are *not* your issue to fix. This can be unbelievably hard to accept, but it's the truth. I know you love your parents and desperately want to help, *but you are not responsible for bailing them out.* Truly owning this perspective will help you make better choices.

Second, if you are on Baby Steps 1–3, recognize that you're not in a position to help anyone out financially. Just like on an airplane, you have to put the oxygen mask on yourself before you can help others. Build a solid financial foundation for your family, then you can think about if and how you can help others. During Baby Steps 1–3, I encourage you to talk about your situation with your parents. Tell them you're getting your money in order too, so you're not able to help them financially. Instead, ask them to go on the Baby Steps journey with you. Recommend they go to the library to check out one of the books we offer. Show them how to download podcasts from the Ramsey Network. All of this is free! The truth is, it's never too late for them to learn something new and rebuild their finances. I met a couple in their eighties who had just paid off all of their debt and completely turned their financial lives around. Your parents can do this, and you can be their biggest encourager and cheerleader even without giving them money.

Third, if you're in a position to help—meaning you're on Baby Steps 4–7—you and your spouse need to be in agreement about how you're going to help. This is a *really* important step. If you and your spouse can't agree on a plan, don't just decide to do something on your own and go do it. You don't want to put your own marriage at risk to help someone else fix their mistake. Either find a way to do this together or work to understand your spouse's point of view. Whatever the decision, it should bring the two of you closer, not drive a wedge between you. If you aren't married, you obviously don't need to be in agreement with your spouse. But do consider running your thoughts past an objective third party who can help you think through the options clearly.

Fourth, make a clear plan and overcommunicate it to your parents. Sometimes you can just give money to a parent without it doing long-term harm. Sometimes, though, you need to offer your help with some strings attached. For example, maybe you and your spouse decide to cover your parents' mortgage for three months and match their savings for an emergency fund *if* they go through *Financial Peace University* and work the plan. The point is to truly help them long term and not enable harmful, ongoing behavior that continues to sink them. They need to learn how to budget. They need to learn the best way to pay off debt. They need to know *how* to take control of their money.

Once you determine the plan in dollar amount, time, and expectations, communicate it clearly and kindly—and probably more than once. Write it all down in black and white. Do whatever it takes so everyone is on the same page. I know this all may sound crazy, but overcommunicating in this scenario is necessary and wise! Clear, communicated boundaries are the biggest blessing for relationships.

Fifth, check on their progress. Are they doing what they said they would do? If so, awesome! Keep encouraging and cheerleading their progress! If not, you'll need to talk to them about what you're seeing and put into motion those consequences. I know this will be painful, and it sounds like you're being the parent in the situation, but you're helping them have better information and make better decisions with their money.

Imagine what would have happened to the couple in their forties who were deep in debt if her parents had required them to learn new money habits instead of just bailing them out. Imagine if they had learned to budget and stay away from debt. They wouldn't be in the same situation they are today—for the second time! Requiring someone's participation isn't punishment. It leads to real growth. Healthy boundaries aren't mean. They protect you and ensure that the person you want to help is truly helped in the long run.

GRACE AND TRUTH IN MY LIFE

There are some really hilarious rumors out there about my dad and our family—how we teach people to pay with cash but still use credit cards or have declared bankruptcy recently. It cracks me up because these rumors get started by people who clearly don't know us.

One of my favorites was when a friend of my dad's, a local police officer, called him up laughing one day and said, "Dave, someone just told me your Viper got repossessed."

"Cool!" my dad said.

His friend said, "Wait. Cool? What do you mean?"

And my dad replied, "I didn't know I owned a Viper!"

You guys, if you knew me or my family personally, you would know we are totally sold on the Baby Steps. I believe in the money principles I teach to the core of who I am. I believe with all my heart they are the best way for all of us to handle our money. In fact, I believe this so deeply I've made it my life's mission to help other people discover these principles and encourage those who are living them! But I can tell you, even though I believe in our teaching *1,000* percent, I do not let it affect the relationships in my life.

Winston and I are on the same page with money. But otherwise I've learned not to take offense when others don't follow the Baby Steps. If a friend pulls out her credit card at dinner to pay the bill, I don't judge her or freak out or start lecturing her. In fact, it happens more frequently than you might guess!

And believe it or not, most members of the extended Ramsey family don't follow the Baby Steps. There are even times when they look at us like we've grown four heads. And you know how much it turns my world upside down or changes the way I feel about them? Not a bit. I love them dearly and want the world for them, *but* I'm only responsible for me. So we get together for holidays and celebrations and have a marvelous time without any judgment. That's what I want for you too! Living according to grace and truth, having healthy boundaries—this, my friend, is what freedom looks like.

As we wrap up part 1 of this book, I want you to think through ways to improve your response to money mistakes. Being too hard on yourself and others won't help, and neither will going too easy. For the best outcome, you're going to need to find a way to bring together grace and truth. Look for ways to do that before the next money mistake happens (because it's coming!). If you'll do that now, when money mistakes do happen, you'll be prepared to face them in a way that heals and restores both your money and your relationships.

NOW IT'S YOUR TURN

1. When money mistakes happen, is your first instinct to give too much grace or not enough?
2. What's the most recent money mistake you've made? On a scale of one to ten, how would you rate the amount of grace you extended yourself, if one is ignoring the problem (enabling) and ten is offering no grace (legalistic)?
3. Think of a time when your spouse, loved one, or close friend made a money mistake that affected you. How would you rate the grace you extended to them on the same one-to-ten scale?
4. Think about your relationships with your parents, siblings, children, and close friends. Do you feel resentment toward them? If you do, where can you put better boundaries in place? If so, do it! Creating healthy boundaries is one of the best things you can do for yourself and your family.

PART 2

Discovering What You *Do* with Money and Why

CHAPTER 9

What Motivates You to *Spend* Money

Part 1 of this book explores your personal money mindset—your childhood money classroom, your unique money tendencies, your money fears, and how you respond to money mistakes. Now we're going to look at what you *do* with that information and apply it to your money.

When Winston and I teach our kids about money, we use three simple principles: give, save, and spend. So for every dollar they earn, they're going to give some, save some, and spend some. When you stop to think about it, that's really all that any of us can do with our money. What's interesting, though, is that these simple principles of giving, saving, and spending are anything but simple. Because while the math may be black and white, the reasons why we do what we do can be very gray. That's why in the next three sections we're going to dive into each principle to discover why you *spend* money the way you do, why you *save* money the way you do, and why you *give* money the way you do. We'll start in this chapter with why you spend money the way you do.

WHY YOU BUY WHAT YOU BUY

It's a given: We all have to buy stuff. Spending money is how we survive in today's world. But have you ever stopped to ask yourself why you buy what you buy? As you continue discovering why you handle money the way you do, one of the most important questions to ask yourself is, *What motivates me to make the purchases I do?*

Think about the clothes you buy, that car you *needed* to drive, the furniture in your home, the toys for your kids, the vacations you take—even the food you get at the grocery store and which grocery store you shop at. Why do you buy what you buy? What motivates your decision to purchase something? Is it something you truly want, or is it because of what others will think? This is the spending scale.

The Spending Scale

LOVING YOUR LIFE	◄————►	IMPRESSING OTHERS

When you're loving *your* life, you're making choices based on what's best for you and your family. When you're loving someone else's life, you're making choices based on what others will think. Spending money for yourself in this context isn't selfish. Spending money for *you* means being true to your unique purpose and values—what moves you, what's important to you, what unique gifts you bring to the world. And just like all the scales, this one isn't fixed. We grow as people over time. So where you were five years ago is likely different from where you are today.

As you look at your own life, begin thinking about where you fall on the spending scale. Are you more satisfied with your purchase when someone else sees it and comments on it, or did you purchase that item purely for your own enjoyment because it will serve you and your family? How do you know? The unexpected truth is that two people can buy the exact same thing, and it can be a healthy purchase for one person and an unhealthy purchase for another. They can both save up and pay cash for an item. But in this case, it's not about the *what* or the *how*; it's about the *why*.

This is a pretty convicting section of the book for me to write, because the truth is, there are plenty of times I spend money for the wrong reasons. I can very easily slip into a spending pattern where I'm buying something to either impress other people or simply because it feels good to buy it. I tell myself that I really need a new shirt for work, but the truth is I have plenty of shirts in my closet already.

As you're considering where you fall on the spending scale, also think back on what you've learned so far about where you fall on some of the other scales. If money is more about status for you than security, you will often fall on the "other people" side of the spending scale. If you're a saver, you don't get a pass on this chapter—you still need to reflect on what motivates you to spend. If you have an abundance mindset, it's probably easier for you to spend without giving it as much thought. If your parents were overly materialistic and you fear ending up like them, you may overreact in your spending choices by automatically disliking what others like just because it's trendy. Your personal money mindset from part 1 has everything to do with how you spend money.

WHAT IT LOOKS LIKE TO LOVE
SOMEONE ELSE'S LIFE

Once upon a time, I didn't believe I really cared about what other people thought. Turns out I do. When Winston and I would take the kids out to eat, I'd often become preoccupied with what other people might be thinking of our parenting based on our kids' behavior. I wanted my kids to sit quietly, look the waiter in the eye, and order their food with a "please" and "thank you." I thought my motivation for having high standards was pure. I thought it was about making others in the restaurant comfortable. But if that were true, why was I the one getting upset when things didn't go perfectly? I'd get so frustrated and even embarrassed.

When I began to reflect on the *why* behind my actions, I realized I was self-conscious when I was in public with my kids. Of course, it's true that no one wants to be around loud, unruly kids. But as I reflected on why I felt edgy, I realized I wanted other people to approve of me as a parent. The motivation behind my behavior—my *why*—was off.

This was a big realization. At that point I had to decide what was really important to me. For me, the goal is for our kids to learn good manners, be respectful of other people, and grow in their level of self-control. It's for *their* good, not for the approval of perfect strangers. When an evening out doesn't go well (and of course that happens because our kids aren't robots), it really *is* okay.

Does it matter if complete strangers approve of my parenting? No—because that literally makes no real difference. Does that mean we let our kids run around a restaurant like wild animals? Of course not. But my motivation and my attitude have shifted. I don't have this down perfectly, but I'm aware of my *why* now, and I work to reframe my motivation when it's off.

Here's the thing about seeking the approval of others: It's not all bad. When I talked to Dr. Chip Dodd about it, he said, "The need to belong and the need to matter are the two most powerful needs a human being has. We're either going to belong and matter as God created us, or we're going to be controlled by other people's opinions." So the need to belong—the need to gain other people's approval—isn't wrong in and of itself. From how we parent to what we drive and wear and eat, we want to be accepted and have people think we're doing a good job in life. It's part of the human condition. But if we're not careful, our desire to belong can impact how we spend our money and what we spend it on in ways that hurt us.

Like a lot of the other tendencies we've explored, there's an unhealthy extreme we have to guard against: caring *too much* about what others think. When our spending decisions are controlled by other people's opinions, we lose out and our wallets do too. We can't let our desire to fit in and please others drive our decision-making. Self-aware adults who want to win with money care less about what other people think and more about staying true to their values.

FEAR OF MAN

My dad says one of the best unintended gifts of the bankruptcy for him was that it removed what he calls his "fear of man," or caring too much about what other people think. Once you've hit rock bottom and have nothing left to lose, you stop caring what other people think. I'll give you an example.

My dad was always a car guy, and before the bankruptcy, he'd bought a really nice Jaguar. He would tell you today that he bought that Jaguar so other people would be impressed. He wanted them to think he was successful and important.

Now fast-forward to today. My dad is still a car guy. But now when he buys a car (with cash, of course), he doesn't care if anyone notices or thinks well of him. His fear of man is gone. He buys the car for himself because he enjoys cars and he can afford it. His spending choices are for *him* now.

Fear of man is the unhealthy side of trying to fit in or keep up or look impressive to others. Fear of man makes you say stuff like:

"I'll buy a luxury car I can't afford so people will think I'm doing well."

"If that's the stroller she uses, then it's the one I have to have."

"If I carry that purse, people will think I'm successful."

"If he's buying a house this year, then so should I."

"They go to Disney every year. We should too."

"If I have a ring that big, other people will be impressed."

Fear of man is making choices for your life based on what other people think or do. And it's a spending cycle that never ends. The lie is that we can gain approval and acceptance by having nice things, but what's "in style" and fashionable keeps changing. New cars come out, home décor trends change, and fashions go out of style. There are always new phones, new watches, nicer luggage, more exotic vacations, and sheets with a higher thread count. You can never cross the finish line of approval—because the finish line keeps moving. Talk about exhausting!

It's also a life that ends up being empty because you're trying to find your worth and identity in people and stuff that cannot give it to you. Internationally renowned pastor and author Henri Nouwen says it like this:

> As long as I keep running about asking: "Do you love me? Do you really love me?" I give all power to the voices of the world and put myself in bondage because the world is filled with "ifs." The world says: "Yes, I love you *if* you are good-looking, intelligent, and wealthy. I love you *if* you have a good education, a good job, and good connections. I love you *if* you produce much, sell much, and buy much." . . . The world's love is and always will be conditional. As long as I keep looking for my true self in the world of conditional love, I will remain "hooked" to the world—trying, failing, and trying again. It is a world that fosters addictions because what it offers cannot satisfy the deepest craving of my heart.[18]

The endless "ifs" and constant chasing after the approval of others lead nowhere. You end up exhausted, feeling lost, and living a life that's not yours. And the craziest part is the thing you were chasing wasn't even real to begin with.

IS THAT ALL THERE IS?

We're surrounded by people who have things that we don't—our family, friends, and all those feeds we scroll through on social media. When we see all that stuff, it's really easy to start thinking that we need or deserve those things too. But what we often forget is that most people are living way beyond their means.

One of my all-time favorite television shows is *Friends*—that classic '90s sitcom about six twenty-somethings living in New York City. I'm such a fan that I had it on my bucket list to visit the set and sit on the famous orange couch in Central Perk, the fictional coffee shop featured in almost every episode of *Friends*. If you're a fan of the show, you probably know it wasn't filmed in New York, but on a movie lot in Los Angeles. I travel pretty regularly to L.A. for work, so Winston decided to come along with me a few years ago. (This was before we had kids.) I booked the two of us a tour of the Warner Bros. lot. I could not wait to get my picture on the famous Central Perk couch. And I did, but I got more out of that tour than I bargained for.

After seeing the sound stage where *Friends* was filmed, our tour continued by tram, taking us through a bunch of sets from other shows. At one point we stopped right in front a house. I recognized it immediately. It was Ross and Monica Geller's parents' house! I turned to Winston and reminded him that one of my favorite scenes from *Friends* took place there. It was a flashback scene, and it featured Monica and Rachel getting ready for prom night in high school. When Rachel's date didn't show up, she was really upset. Monica's older brother, Ross, saw Rachel get upset, so he put on a tux, intending to take Rachel (the love of his life) to the prom. Right as he is coming down the stairs in his tux, Rachel's date shows up. Monica, Rachel, and their dates all rush out the door, leaving Ross heartbroken on the stairs. All you *Friends* fans know exactly what I'm talking about!

After this flashback, the scene switches back to all the friends gathered in present day, watching this prom scene on an old home video. Right then, Rachel walks over to Ross and gives him a long-awaited kiss. At that moment, a million women in America screamed, because that's what we'd all been waiting for! I mean, it is just the *best*.

So there I was, with my husband, about to go into the house where one of my favorite scenes from my favorite show was filmed. The production team had done a great job making the outside of the house inviting and realistic. I walked in the front door of the "house," and I was shocked. My mind scrambled to make sense of it. Even though the outside looked like a normal house, there was nothing inside except for a staircase. It was so bare. My *Friends*-loving heart was deeply disappointed. Logically, I knew Monica, Ross, and Rachel wouldn't be inside, but still, somehow I'd thought there'd be some sign of familiarity from the show. I soon learned that many of the scenes that seemed to be "inside" that house were actually filmed on sound stages blocks away. I turned to Winston and said, "Is that all there is?"

These days I frequent that Warner Bros. lot because I'm a guest on a show that films there. Every time I go, I drive through what looks like an old western town—a general store, a saloon, the whole nine yards. It's incredibly realistic, like a cowboy might come out any minute and start a gunfight. But now I know better. There's nothing inside those realistic-looking buildings. They're just façades. All those different sets and buildings are fake.

Façades

Hollywood isn't the only place you'll find fake fronts. They're all around us: the people we work with, our neighbors, those we go to church with, even us! Everyone looks great on the outside, like they have it all together—but it's often only a fake front paid for with debt. The façade is supposed to give an impression of success, of having "arrived." But open the door to their lives and there's only a staircase inside. We've been comparing our own lives to something that isn't even real! And that's where the danger comes in.

American households with credit card debt carry an average balance of just over $14,500.[19] They're literally living paycheck to paycheck in order to finance a lifestyle they can't afford. That big SUV in the driveway and their designer jeans may send the signal that they have it all together, but statistics tell us they don't. So what ends up happening when you compare your life to your neighbor's? You're often comparing your life to broke people—and aspiring to be like people who are broke is a terrible plan.

In 2016, I wrote a book called *Love Your Life, Not Theirs* about our comparison culture and how it affects our money habits. What's crazy, though, is that since the book released, the issue has only gotten worse. I know this because the subject continues to come up when I'm speaking with guests on my show or during interviews when I'm traveling around the country. Comparison is such a sneaky thing and can impact our spending decisions (and a lot of other things) before we even know it's happening.

When we compare our lives to how other people are living, we're not only comparing ourselves to people who often can't afford the life they're living, but we're also comparing ourselves only to the parts of their life they want us to see. It's often a lie—*and yet comparison often drives us to buy and do things we wouldn't normally buy or do.*

The New York Times featured a story in 2019 about two newlywed couples on their respective honeymoons. One couple went to Aruba for their honeymoon. The groom said, "The thing I remember most about my honeymoon was the sunsets, but not because of their beauty. It was like a photo shoot for some magazine that would never exist." He talked about the week-long trip as a "sunset nightmare," "stressful," and "torturous." That's because the bride reported feeling pressure to prove to the world she was having a great time. So she spent most days shooting, editing, or planning her Instagram posts. She ignored her new husband because she was trying to show folks thousands of miles away she was having a good time. And this is not uncommon. The new bride said she even chose her food based on if it would look cute on Instagram. The worst part is that even though she noticed her husband was unhappy, she didn't let his mood get between her and the good sunset shot. Suffice it to say, the article states they almost separated after that trip: "Not because of the honeymoon alone, but it was pretty bad."[20]

The second couple in the article had a similar story. Because social media typically portrays the best parts of everyone's life, sometimes our expectations of what life should look like get completely out of control. This couple had originally planned to travel to the English countryside—something they were both really excited to do. But when people started asking the soon-to-be bride where they were going on their honeymoon, she said no one seemed impressed by the English countryside.

So, feeling pressure to choose a honeymoon destination that *sounded* magical and impressive, they ditched two weeks in the country for Italy instead. It cost more to go to Italy, so they had to book a shorter trip. Then they ended up in an Italian apartment without air conditioning. "The bed was on a mezzanine with a sloping ceiling so neither of us could stand up straight," she said. "We didn't have sex the entire time we were there, because it was so hot and you couldn't move fully and I was too cross about the apartment."[21]

This makes me so sad! These couples made significant once-in-a-lifetime choices based completely on what their "followers" and "friends" on social media might think. In an effort to keep up with the Joneses, these couples missed their own honeymoons! And while these are pretty extreme examples, the reality is, this is what happens when we live and spend for the approval of others. If we're not careful, we'll lose sight of what we want and sacrifice our real life for a virtual one.

How to Guard Against Spending for Others

If you find yourself on this side of the spending scale more often than not (guilty!), I want to pass along some questions I've learned to ask myself before I buy something. These questions will help you spend money more thoughtfully and save more money too.

1. If no one ever sees this purchase, do I still want it?
2. If I don't post about it on social media, do I still want it?
3. If it gets ruined, how will that affect me?
4. Do I believe I will be fulfilled after making this purchase?
5. Do I believe this thing is going to make me happy?

Asking these questions will give you a quick gut check about your motive for wanting to make that purchase. And let me tell you, these questions have convicted me more than once to *not* buy something I thought I had to have!

If you ask these questions and your answers tell you that you're buying an item for others more than yourself, just wait on the purchase. It doesn't mean you can't ever buy that item. It just means you need to get in the right head space first. You're going to make the best spending decision when the motivation behind it is right.

It's also important to remember it's okay to have nice stuff—just don't let your nice stuff have you. How does that happen? It happens when you draw your identity from your stuff—like thinking, *I'm awesome because I'm wearing these brand-name jeans*—and when you buy something just to impress other people, like my dad did when he bought that first Jaguar. And it can also happen when you go into debt to make a purchase. When you don't own an item in full, that thing owns a piece of you emotionally and financially. So once you get to a healthy spot emotionally to make a purchase, make sure you also have the money to pay for it too. Debt makes loving your life very difficult.

Also, be sure to give yourself grace. There are seasons when I'm really focused on doing what's best for my family, and then

I'll slip and find myself spending for the approval of others. The goal is to notice when it happens. We're not going to get it perfect all the time. The key is growth.

Now, there's one other thing I want you to consider. The only thing that's going to permanently shift your motivation for spending is a heart change. No amount of budgeting or math will affect you that deeply—but experiencing the power of contentment can.

THE POWER OF CONTENTMENT

Contentment is a process that changes your motivation for spending money. How? By changing what you value. Instead of valuing the acquisition of more stuff, you value other things more. I've written more extensively about contentment in *Love Your Life, Not Theirs* and *The Contentment Journal*, but here's how it works: It starts with gratitude, which develops into humility, and over time grows into contentment. And believe me, it works! This process has changed my life.

Contentment is the opposite of spending money because of other people. It's about being satisfied with your life right now where God has you versus feeling like you have to keep up. It's about having peace in your heart for the season of life you're in and knowing your life is meant for something meaningful. Instead of chasing after the next new shiny thing, contentment changes your heart to be satisfied with what you already have. So how do you grow contentment? It starts with cultivating a habit of gratitude.

Studies have shown that people who start their days off with gratitude have high levels of satisfaction in their lives.[22] Begin a gratitude habit by writing down three things you're grateful for when you wake up each day. That's it! You can be grateful for big things—like the support of a good friend or a job you love—but it's also the little stuff, like writing with your favorite pen or getting to start the morning with your favorite cup of coffee. I started this practice years ago, and this one simple act changed not just my day, but eventually my outlook on life. Gratitude is unbelievably powerful.

As you build a daily habit of gratitude and look for things you're thankful for, humility grows. True humility is not humiliation. You don't have to put yourself down or devalue your life in order to be humble. Bestselling author and pastor Rick Warren said, "Humility is not thinking less of yourself, it is thinking of yourself less." Humility is considering others more. The more your heart grows in gratitude, the more you start seeing the people around you—not for their approval—but because you really care about them. It's valuing who they are and who God made them to be. Humility breeds a life of kindness, generosity, joy, and fulfillment. And after humility grows is when contentment really shows up.

When you take the time to lay a strong foundation of gratitude and humility, contentment becomes a part of who you are. It's not just a momentary feeling; it's part of your character. Contentment isn't laziness. It's not being a doormat. It's not being aimless. You'll still be working hard to crush the goals in your life. Being content has more to do with your *why*—living life on your terms—not with what you have. You can be content with a little and you can be content with a lot. The Bible says, "Godliness with contentment is great gain" (1 Timothy 6:6). That's so true! Contentment *is* great gain.

Content people spend their money thoughtfully. Content people sacrifice their lifestyle to get out of debt and experience financial peace. They save money and give more. Contentment changes what you value most and helps you curb unhealthy spending. The more you practice gratitude, humility, and contentment, the more your spending will become less about impressing others and more about what's truly important to you.

WHAT IT LOOKS LIKE TO LOVE *YOUR* LIFE

We've looked at one side of the spending scale, now let's talk about the other: what it looks like to love your own life—to spend money for *you* and not anyone else.

Now remember, when I talk about spending money for yourself, I'm not talking about satisfying every whim you have to get the latest and greatest of everything. Spending money for you is being true to your unique purpose and values. In other words, when you're loving your life, you're paying more attention to your world than anyone else's. Spending money for yourself means you're content with what you have and intentionally living out what's important to you. I'll give you an example.

I have some friends who were moving across the country for work. Before the move, they lived in a larger single-family home with a big backyard and gorgeous views. It was a beautiful house, but they had come to realize that they bought it because that's what other people expected. It was just "what everybody does" but not what they really wanted.

After spending time reflecting on their values, they realized what was most important to them was saving more money and spending more time together as a family. So when they moved, they decided to buy a smaller townhouse. Their decision not only saved them money, but now that they have less square footage and almost no outside maintenance, they also have more free time together as a family. Now, am I saying everyone needs to downsize to a townhouse? Of course not. The whole point of spending money for yourself is determining what's important to *you*.

When you spend money for you and not others, you're motivated to spend mindfully, according to a deeper *why* that's based on your unique values and purpose. I'm going to guess your personal mission in life isn't to help people take control of their money. That's in *my* DNA! You may have a passion for teaching young children or crunching numbers or advocating for endangered wildlife. Your purpose may be to discover the cure for a disease or write a moving novel or raise incredible kids. We're all made to do something meaningful, and that should be what informs how we spend our money—not impressing our neighbors.

When you're spending money for you, your *why* will help you decide what is and isn't a good purchase. It will no longer matter, for example, how much a mortgage company will loan you for a house—it only matters what truly fits you and serves your family. Knowing your *why* will help you make the hard spending choices, like cutting expenses in order to get out of debt so you'll be in a position to live out your purpose. It also provides a filter for making the fun spending choices like buying nice knives for your kitchen because you worked hard, saved that money, and cooking is your passion. And it helps you live generously, spending money in a way that serves others. When you buy according to your *why*, there's rarely any regrets, buyer's remorse, or overwhelming fear of that thing getting damaged. Your purchases don't have a grip on you. Your mood doesn't dictate what you buy. It's a whole new level of freedom with your money.

Do you know what your *why* is? If you don't immediately know what's most important to you, I encourage you to spend some time thinking about it. In order to win with money, you need to know what you value most. Start by asking questions like:

- What moves you?
- Who and what matters most to you?
- What will you regret *not* doing?
- What unique gifts do you bring to the world?

As you dig into these questions, you'll begin to see a general idea of your values and purpose. Then hold on to those ideas. We'll keep exploring them in the next two chapters.

When your motive for spending money is to live a life you've chosen and love, that "fear of man" we talked about earlier is replaced by something different. As a person of faith, I call it the fear of God. Oswald Chambers said, "The remarkable thing about God is that when you fear God, you fear nothing else. Whereas if you do not fear God, you fear everything else."[23] When you know you belong to God, living for other people loses its power over you. When pleasing God is the most important thing to you, the pressure to keep up disappears. There are no moving finish lines to cross, no approval boxes to check. You can be fulfilled and at peace because your identity and worth come from an unchanging God. *This is true freedom.* Whether you're a person of faith or not, your quality of life increases exponentially when you let go of trying to please others and live instead according to what's most important to you.

YOUR SECRET SPENDING WEAPON

As we talk about spending money for you, there's one very big temptation you need to guard against: spending money just because it feels good. This is so easy to do in our culture. Have something to celebrate? Go to dinner! Had a bad day? Treat yourself! Someone you love feeling down? Buy them a little something to brighten their day. We lovingly call it "retail therapy." Someone once laughingly told me, "It's cheaper than actual therapy!" But is it?

When you start scrolling on your phone and adding things to your cart, there's a chemical reaction inside your brain that can actually become addicting, and it has been proven that people spend money as a coping mechanism to avoid pain. Thirty-one percent of women say they've shopped to improve their mood, and 53 percent of people have shopped to celebrate something.[24] It's a lot like getting a runner's high. When you run, dopamine is released, which causes feelings of pleasure and satisfaction. The *same* thing happens when you shop—but it often results in wasting money on things you really don't care about.

Part of guarding against emotional spending is to spend on purpose. That means, before you make a purchase, do a quick gut check about your motives . . . *and then pull out your budget!* Budgeting is something I talk about all the time, but it can also help you if you have a tendency to shop because it feels good. Your budget will tell you honestly if you have money to spend and if shopping is part of your overall financial plan for the month. It acts like a stop sign in a moment of weakness when all you can hear is, "I need to buy this!" If you look at your budget, have the money, and it's something you planned on buying, go for it. If it's not, pay attention to the stop sign. It's there to protect you.

When it comes to spending—whether in general or to lift your mood—you have three secret weapons: (1) spending for you and no one else, (2) living in alignment with your *why*, and (3) making and sticking to your budget. If you'll do these three things, you'll stay true to who you are and keep your spending on track for the long haul.

NOW IT'S YOUR TURN

1. Look back at your bank account and review the purchases you made last month. Are there any categories where you overspent because you were shopping to impress other people?
2. Where would you put yourself on the spending scale and why?
3. Based on your unique values and purpose, what is your deeper *why*? How can you begin to incorporate that into your daily spending?
4. What are three things you're grateful for right now? In order to avoid the comparison trap, commit to writing down three things you're thankful for every day.

CHAPTER 10

What Motivates You to *Save* Money

Now that we've explored why we *spend* money the way we do, let's talk about its opposite: why we *save* (and don't save) money. Like we talked about in part 1, people are naturally either savers or spenders. You natural savers may not think you need this section of the book. But hold tight—there's more to saving than you might think. And spenders, I promise this won't be a boring chapter on saving. It's actually going to set you up to spend money on the things you really value.

A lot of us think about saving all wrong. It feels boring or like a burden, an added expense you can't afford, or something that stands in the way of what you want right now. We forget that saving money is actually a joy. You *get* to save a portion of every dollar you make for yourself and your future! Aside from saving up your emergency fund, when you're saving, you're typically saving for one of your dreams: something you want to experience or buy or do. Seeing your savings account grow—knowing all that money is going toward something you want—is actually a lot of fun! So why is it that so many of us miss this? Because we don't understand the connection between saving and dreaming.

That's why in this chapter on saving, we're going to do something you might not expect: We're going to talk about how you dream. Because how you dream has everything to do with how you save.

THE CONNECTION BETWEEN SAVING AND DREAMING

We all have excuses or reasons why we don't save. I hear them all the time in my work. Let's look at the most common reasons for not saving and what's really at the root of them all:

1. You don't make enough money.
2. You spend more than you earn.
3. You're weighed down by debt.
4. You grew up in a money classroom that makes saving seem impossible or unimportant.

Do any of these sound familiar? Do you struggle to make ends meet each month, let alone put savings away for an emergency? Is savings even on your radar? These reasons can sound reasonable, but let's take a closer look at what's really going on.

One of my friends grew up in the Unaware Classroom. Her parents never talked about the importance of saving money, so she never worried about doing it. She had made a decent salary as a writer her entire career, but after a decade, she had nothing to show for it—no savings at all. Then one day she had a medical emergency that put her thousands of dollars in debt. She didn't know that could even happen until those bills started rolling in. As she faced the reality of what it would take to dig her way out of debt, she knew two things: Her ignorance about not saving was costly, and she never wanted to be in that position again. That's when she realized she needed a plan for her money.

If you're reading this book and don't have any savings, know you're not the only one. Forty-seven percent of Americans have less than $1,000 saved for an emergency.[25] But also know that not having any savings is a warning sign for two big problems. The first problem is that your house isn't in order. You're not prepared. Even if things appear to be going well, if you don't have a plan for your money that includes savings, it's only a matter of time before the unexpected hits and you have a major problem. Life is going to throw you some curve balls: a medical emergency, job loss, the air-conditioning unit goes out, a storm damages your home, you hit a deer on the way to work. Having an emergency fund isn't optional. At some point you're going to need one. If you don't have any savings today, the time to get your house in order is *right now.*

But not having savings is also a warning sign of a second problem: that you're not tuned in to your dreams. Most people don't think about how deeply connected saving and dreaming are. But if you're not saving, it means you're not working toward any of your dreams. You're likely just floating from job to job and city to city instead of steadily working toward something meaningful. And when that happens, it's usually because you have no clue what your dreams are. It's also possible that you might be saving a little here and a little there, but it's going to take tapping into your dreams to see real progress.

Dreams are actually crucial to your financial life because they help you see what you value and motivate you to save for the long haul. Unless you're a die-hard saver, saving for the sake of saving isn't meaningful. But when you really, truly want something, no one can stop you from saving for it and working hard to make it happen. If you want to live out your retirement dreams, you'll happily put away 15 percent of your income each month. If you care deeply about fighting poverty in your city, you'll find more ways to cut your expenses so you can donate regularly. If you dream of adopting a child, you'll sacrifice for years to bring them home. Why? Because saving gives you the freedom to follow your dreams.

DREAMERS AND REALISTS

Now that you know why dreams are so important for saving money, we need to dig into the way you're naturally wired to dream. When it comes to dreaming, we tend to fall into two camps: You're either a dreamer or a realist.

The Saving Scale

| DREAMER | ←→ | REALIST |

As always, neither is good or bad—they're just different. One friend described the difference between a dreamer and a realist as the difference between a train conductor who sets the course for where the train is going and the engine that pulls the cargo and passengers to the right place. A dreamer is the train conductor, while a realist is the engine that gets the train where it's supposed to go. And both are very necessary to get anywhere!

Dreamers

Dreamers are the kind of people who have five new business ideas a day. They're typically abundance-minded people, always willing to try new things. They're the visionaries. They often think about the future and resist the idea that there are limits to what they can do. They think in terms of the big picture rather than focusing on details or executing what needs to be done in order for their dream to happen. If most of these statements sound like you, you're probably a dreamer.

Dreamers, we need you in this world! That said, there are some things you need to be aware of. First, you can't hang out in Dreamer Land all the time. If you do, none of those amazing plans and ideas you have will ever actually happen. You need to bring those ideas down from the clouds and work on them.

Dreamers, you also have to accept that not every idea you have is a good one. I can say this because I'm a dreamer. You're my people! I get you! It requires some humility and maturity to know which ideas are worth pursuing. I have heard more than one woman say, "My husband wants to quit his job to start up this new business, and I think it's a crazy idea!" Then the wife seems like a Debbie Downer because she's not super support-ive—and that's just because she's thinking about all the details it will take and money it will cost to get there.

One woman told me her husband wanted to borrow $200,000 to open a sandwich shop. He had no business plan and no track record of understanding how to run a restaurant. To most everyone, the whole idea sounded foolish. In this situation, the wife wasn't a Debbie Downer—*she was a lifeguard.* She saved both of them from making a massive financial mistake that would take years to recover from.

I'm the dreamer in our marriage. I'll be thinking about the future and within five minutes of daydreaming want to book a quick weekend trip on a whim. The dream of getting out of town and doing something spontaneous is so exciting to me. I'll start brainstorming and look into places to rent and activities we can do, only to come out of that dream state to realize I've spent time planning a trip we don't need to take with money we don't need to spend. But as a dreamer, those ideas come fast and furious and usually all sound great to me in the moment.

Dreamers and Saving

When it comes to saving, some dreamers will find it easy because they're so committed to their dream. They love their dream so much that they're willing to do anything to work for it—even if it takes two years to save up to buy the tools they need to start a business or to earn a degree to make the new career happen. The more committed you can be to your dream, the easier it will be to do the hard work of achieving it.

But because dreamers *are* in the clouds a lot (because it's so fun to hang out there!), saving money can also be very challenging. One of the main reasons is because dreamers often don't want to wait. They see their dream in all its glory and want to dive in *now*. Stopping to patiently save to make it happen seems impossible. But dreamers, you have to be willing to accept that dreams take time. Be the tortoise, not the hare! The most meaningful things often take years or decades to build. Refusing to accept this will only limit your progress.

It can also be hard for dreamers to save because they have fifteen new ideas every day—and all of them need to be saved up for. But dreamers, you need to keep in mind you only want to pursue the *right* ideas. So how do you know which ones to work on? A strong indicator for me is to pay attention to the ideas that keep coming up. If the same idea continues to pop up, there's usually a reason. Time is another helpful tool in knowing which ideas to pursue, so write down the ideas you have. Whether it's a dream of what school to send your kids to, wanting to adopt, a business idea, anything! Then don't look at the list for a couple of weeks, and come back to it fresh. If it still excites you, maybe that's your cue to start moving toward making it a reality. It's so important to balance your dreamer personality with maturity and patience.

Realists

Realists don't tend to have a thousand ideas or dreams a day. But when they have an idea, it's usually well-thought-out because they naturally put a lot of energy into figuring out the *how*. An idea is presented, they think about it, evaluate it, and see it's a good idea. They get real practical, real quick. How is this going to get done? What needs to happen? How much money do they have to make it possible? How can they do it for less? How long will it take? What information do they need to gather? How do they get help with this? If you tend to look at the details and stay grounded in reality, you're probably a realist. The gift of being a realist is that in many ways, it's easier for you to make a life you love a reality because you're a pro at executing your ideas.

The key for realists, however, is to remember to allow dreams the room to breathe. As a realist, you've probably had some wild dreams of your own that you shut down by thinking, *That's ridiculous! I'll never be able to pull that off.* If your own dream or the dream someone else has doesn't seem realistic the moment you hear it, resist shutting it down immediately. Remember that dreams usually don't appear fully formed. They need work. They need expertise. They need the help of a realist!

As a realist, also understand that you can seem like the killer of all dreams to a dreamer. There's a chance you've gotten in the habit of automatically saying no to any idea the dreamer in your life has. You easily see how this idea is going to happen (or not happen), but your quick assessment can unintentionally hurt your dreamer. They can start to doubt themselves or feel like you don't believe in them. Like I said before, there's a good chance the idea isn't worth pursuing—but you don't want to crush their spirit. So use your powers for good. Be curious. Ask questions. You can be the lifeguard *and* kind and encouraging. And realists, remember that not every dream is unwise. Some really are worth investing in!

Realists and Saving

You might think that all realists would naturally be great at saving, but that's not true. The hard part of saving for some realists is that they get overwhelmed and discouraged. They do the math and realize they have to save $600 a month in order to save up the $7,000 needed for that dream European vacation they want to take in a year. Because they're realists, it just seems like too much—too much money and too much time with too many other competing priorities to juggle. If this is you, remember to take a deep breath. Bill Gates said, "Most people overestimate what they can do in one year and underestimate what they can do in ten years." You can't do it all at once, but you can prioritize what's most important and do one thing at a time. You'll be surprised by how much you can accomplish over time with steady focus.

Other realists *love* to save. It's especially easy for them to save for emergencies because they're always thinking things through, understanding that what can go wrong probably will. The same principle applies to their dreams: Realists can be committed to their dream, have a detailed plan, put it in the budget, and stick to it. They can be wonderfully patient and steadfast as they watch their savings grow. If this is you, lean into this strength of yours. Get more disciplined in it. It will serve you well as you work toward your goals.

Wherever you fall on the dreamer versus realist scale, keep in mind that even though you have a natural tendency for one or the other, we all have to do both tasks. Just like the other scales, your goal here is moderation. We all need to spend time dreaming, and we all need to spend time making a plan for how to accomplish those dreams. We'll talk in chapter 11 about ways to dream and plan, but I want to encourage you to keep working at doing both better. Dreamers, remember: The ideas that keep coming back to you are not by accident. You've probably had plenty of dreams that *didn't* happen—and now you're really grateful for that! But pay close attention to the ones that keep coming back up again and again. Those are the ones you want to work. Realists, use your strength of being grounded and realistic to your advantage!

But don't forget to actually dream about the kind of life you want to create and allow those ideas to breathe and grow. Don't settle for how you've always done it. Be aware of how you're wired, but also keep learning and growing from others.

WHAT STOPS US FROM DREAMING

Just like there are reasons we don't save, there are also reasons we don't dream. Before we explore the different types of dreams that will help you save for what matters most to you, I want us to think about what stops us from dreaming. This is really important because our dreams aren't coincidental or random—*our dreams are part of why we're living on this earth.* I see three big things that keep us from dreaming and saving: the daily grind, the naysayers, and trauma.

The Daily Grind

If you're like me, sometimes you look back at the past week and think, *What just happened?* A lot of days can be a blur. I wake up, maybe have a few minutes of quiet time, and then the kids are up and wanting breakfast. I'm trying to get out the door on time—doing my hair with one hand while putting one girl in her high chair and grabbing cereal for the other one. Then it's time to pack lunches and finish my makeup before kissing them goodbye. I drive to work to attend meetings and, hopefully grab a quick sandwich for lunch. I look up, and it's time to drive back home.

I rush to get dinner ready, all while trying to entertain hungry kids. I get everyone to the table—then try to *keep* everyone at the table. We clean up the kitchen and run baths for the kids. One baby runs out of the bathroom and sprints naked through the house. (Never fails!) So we run to get them and wrestle pajamas on. Then it's time to tuck them in—which, as every parent knows, is a wild card. Some nights are effortless, while others take an hour before they get to sleep. After all that, Winston and I fall back on the couch thinking, *Finally!* Then it's off to bed to catch up on our day and maybe read or watch our favorite show . . . and before I know it, the alarm sounds and we start again.

Now, I'm not complaining! Winston and I have precious, wonderful moments with our kids—but, man, life with little ones can be exhausting. Babies and toddlers just equal physical exhaustion for me. I'll probably look back at these words in a few years and smile because, as we know, life changes and time flies. Before I know it, Winston and I will have teenagers in the house. Our highs and lows will be oh-so different. But today our daily routine is full and demanding, and if we're not careful, it can distract us from dreaming and really living.

Your day-to-day grind might look entirely different, but we all go through seasons when we can get stuck in the routines of life. What you want to watch for is letting time get away from you. You don't want to look up in two years or ten years and realize you haven't been dreaming and saving. The daily grind and its pace can be a daily distraction. Author and philosopher Dallas Willard said you want to "ruthlessly eliminate hurry from your life."[26] Why? Because *hurry* distracts us from real living. (Notice he didn't say *busy*. *Busy* is being engaged in something that requires our time or attention. *Hurry* is going fast.) It's so easy to get caught up in just surviving the day, rushing from one urgent thing to the next, that you completely miss out on building something sweet and meaningful in life. It's worth the effort to stop the frenzy and begin to dream again.

If you fall on the realist side, the daily grind could be a place of safety for you. You can accomplish tasks throughout the day, and it feels like success. While those tasks are important, remember to look at the bigger picture of life and not just what's right in front of you—take some time to dream.

You dreamers out there may lose yourself to dreaming when the daily grind gets stressful or boring. Remember, moderation is key, so make sure to enjoy the life that's right in front of you while you're dreaming about the future.

Naysayers

Even though Pinterest is full of cute, encouraging quotes like, "Dream Big!" and "Follow Your Dreams!" (think hearts and rainbows with pretty, cursive writing), many of us are also told our dreams aren't possible. It can be a parent, teacher, friend, or just someone we look up to. They usually mean well, but their words can stop us dead in our tracks.

Public speaking is part of my job. It has been for well over a decade, and it all started with a not-so-typical job while I was in high school. As a teenager, I would travel around with my dad on the weekends to different cities across America. At the time, he held these events on Saturdays, and they would be packed with anywhere from 5,000 to 12,000 people. These were all-day events, teaching people how to handle their money.

During that time, someone at the company had the idea for me to go out on stage and pitch the kids' products we had. They thought hearing from Dave Ramsey's youngest daughter would be encouraging to parents as they thought about how to teach their own children how money works. I initially resisted the idea, thinking there was no way I could get up in front of that many people. My sister and brother and I grew up working the book tables at these events. Being at the events was pretty normal, but going on stage was a totally foreign idea.

But a few more people got wind of the idea, and after some encouragement, I agreed to do it. With some help, I wrote out a quick, five-minute talk. It covered everything from a "Top Ten" list on how tough it was to be Dave Ramsey's daughter to why it's important to teach kids about money—and the chore charts and money envelopes we used as Ramsey kids were so helpful in making the money lessons stick. I practiced and practiced for the first event of the season. It was in Spokane, Washington, and there were about 6,000 people in the audience that day.

Standing side stage, about to be introduced, I was as nervous as you would imagine a 15-year-old would be. But I walked out there, did my five-minute talk, and felt such relief and even enjoyment as the supportive audience laughed at my jokes in spite of my voice shaking. I remember walking offstage with so much adrenaline. I couldn't believe I had just done something I thought was impossible—and not just done it, but actually had fun.

Right as I walked off the stage, one of the guys who had coached me for the event came over to me, and I'll never forget the first thing he said to me: "You talked really fast." Not, "You did it! Great first try!" Nothing about being courageous for facing 6,000 adults as a teenager. Just, "You talked really fast." It was a simple sentence, but at that moment, my heart sank and I suddenly became very self-conscious. I remember thinking maybe I hadn't done a good job after all and felt myself tear up. His words stung deeply.

The reality is, this happens to all of us. We want to take a risk and try something new, but the words of others can destroy our courage to keep going. As I stood side stage, reeling from this guy's words, others began to come up to me. They were smiling and cheering for me and spoke encouraging words. But what if I had only listened to the negative words? What if I had let that one comment dictate the rest of my life? The truth is, I probably did talk too fast. My first attempt at public speaking wasn't perfect—but that didn't mean I should give up. And the same is true for you. Don't let the voices of other people—or a hurtful, discouraging experience—stop you from pursuing your dreams.

Naysayers aren't always external voices either. We can do it to ourselves—and it's probably more damaging than anything anyone else could ever say to us. I have had to work through that internal voice at work, as a wife, and as a mom. When I feel like I'm not measuring up or that my dream is impossible, it's easy to get stuck in that cycle of "naysaying" myself. As you give yourself permission and space to dream, you may hear a voice in your head that says, *You don't need that. You're being greedy. Don't be selfish.* Or you may hear, *There's no way you can do that! It's too big of a dream. You're being ridiculous. You will never have the money to do that.* Let's address that voice.

This voice comes in many forms, but its mission is always to stop us from doing what matters. In *The War of Art*, Steven Pressfield calls our internal naysayer "Resistance." He says,

> Most of us have two lives. The life we live, and the unlived life within us. Between the two stands Resistance. . . . Have you ever wanted to be a mother, a doctor, an advocate for the weak and helpless; to run for office, crusade for the

planet, campaign for world peace, or to preserve the environment? Late at night have you experienced a vision of the person you might become, the work you could accomplish, the realized being you were meant to be? Are you a writer who doesn't write, a painter who doesn't paint, an entrepreneur who never starts a venture? Then you know what Resistance is. . . . [Resistance] prevents us from achieving the life God intended when He endowed each of us with our own unique genius.[27]

Resistance is there every day to keep us from achieving our dreams. And its message is one we can wrongly take to heart, believing it's true.

"There's no way I can do that."

"Saving for that dream is impossible."

"That's just crazy. I've got to be realistic. My children are depending on me."

The one solitary goal of Resistance is to keep you from achieving what you're meant to achieve. If we allow it, our internal voice alone can destroy our chances to create a life we love. You guys, the stakes of *not* dreaming, of *not* pursuing what's important to us, are crazy high. Dreaming isn't for the faint of heart. When we dream, we're digging into our very purpose for living. So be alert and stay focused through this process. It's going to be worth it.

Trauma

Before we move on, let me say something to those of you who have recently experienced trauma or are recovering from past trauma. Maybe you're going through a divorce, suffered abuse, or someone you dearly love has passed away. Whatever it is—first,

I'm so, so sorry. Truly. I cannot imagine how difficult it's been for you.

If you've suffered recent trauma or experienced childhood trauma, dreaming can be difficult to do on your own. But what I find really hopeful is that learning to dream is a skill. And a skill is something *anyone* can choose to learn over time. Learning to dream is also something that a mental health professional or pastor can help you with. So when you're able, find a trusted friend or professional to sit with you, in person if possible, and slowly guide you in relearning how to dream.

Also, as you start dreaming again, be prepared for your new dreams to look both the same and different as they did before. If you've been dreaming of pursuing a new career for years, you may still want to do that. How you achieve that dream may be different now, but the dream is still the same. Or your priorities may have shifted significantly, and you now realize you *don't* want to invest your time and money preparing for that career. It's okay to let go of old dreams and create new ones. The big idea here is to dream. Don't stop doing that because of what you're going through or have gone through. Start small if you need to— just keep dreaming!

Now that you understand the connection between saving and dreaming and know more about your dreamer or realist self, let's dig into the different types of dreams that reveal what's most important to you.

CHAPTER 11

Discovering What's Most Important to You

When you think about the future, what do you want to see happen? What's important to you? What do you love and value? When you're eighty, what will you regret *not* doing? Start thinking about it without editing yourself. There will be plenty of time later to make changes. Just write it down for now. Focus on the things you're willing to work for. And as you start thinking about what your dreams are, I want you to think in three different categories: short term, long term, and shared. These three categories will help you both discover what's most important to you and prioritize what you do when.

Short-Term Dreams

I'm all for big dreams! That said, they're not all doable right away, so I want to encourage you to think about dreams in the short term separately from dreams in the long term. Short-term dreams are obtainable in two years or less. Anything longer, I consider a long-term dream. Short-term dreams are exciting because they're attainable in the near future. If you're more of a realist, you'll likely love short-term dreams because the steps are clearly defined with less room for ambiguity. If you're more of a dreamer, you'll love short-term dreams because they will give you quick wins. Some examples of short-term dreams are:

1. Take your kids to experience a national park.
2. Get out of debt so you get to keep *all* of your income.
3. Move to a different home.
4. Stay home with your kids and homeschool them.
5. Travel to a country you've always wanted to explore.
6. Start painting again and sell your art.

The powerful thing about short-term dreams is that they're like fuel. They usually cost less money to accomplish, and—because they're quicker to achieve—they're super motivating. You can also see pretty easily the steps involved in making short-term dreams a reality, including what sacrifices you'll need to make. If you're just cutting expenses for the heck of it, you can run out of steam quickly because there's no light at the end of the tunnel. But when you're aiming for something you care about, the hard work and sacrifices are bearable—even energizing.

Maybe you're saving like crazy to go to the beach. You're six months out, and you want to hit a certain number in your bank account in order to cash flow the trip. Cutting your restaurant budget in half for the next six months may not sound like a good time, but man, you're going to eat well and have a blast at the beach! Or maybe you've always wanted to learn how to bake beautiful tarts and pies. Signing up for a culinary class will mean devoting one night a week to learning the basics of baking. Plus, you'll have to practice in order to get it right. (Can I volunteer as taste tester?) But it'll be so worth it to get to serve amazing desserts to friends and family. Whatever the sacrifice is or money you need to save—when you're doing it for something better, you have hope and motivation that keeps you driving forward.

Winston and I recently finished saving for a short-term dream. We knew we wanted to get a new car once our third baby came into the picture, and I had my eye on that new minivan I talked about earlier. That's right! As a mom with three kids, a minivan was my dream car. I can hear the haters now—"that's not a cool mom car!"—but let me tell you, this van has more bells and whistles than my old SUV did—and for way less! And don't even get me started on the seats that move side to side for the kids to get in and out quickly, plus automatic doors and more. (I could be a minivan saleswoman in a different life!) This was a short-term dream that required some discipline to save what we needed. We had to say no to some fun things in order to say yes to the van, but I'm so grateful we did because now I get to enjoy it every single day.

Long-Term Dreams

Long-term dreams take longer than two years to achieve either because they're larger in scope (like paying off your house) or because they happen later in life (like saving for retirement). Also, long-term dreams often include what I call your "so that." You want to build wealth *so that* you have the freedom to pursue the projects most important to you. You want to build wealth *so that* you can build a school for a village in a developing country.

You want to build wealth *so that* you can pay for your children's college education. Again, paying off debt isn't the ultimate goal here. Building wealth isn't even our end game. You want to pay off debt and build wealth *so that* you can live life on your own terms.

Now obviously, it usually costs a lot more to save for long-term dreams than it does for short-term dreams. If you're a realist, long-term dreams can give you a sense of relief because time is on your side to accomplish them. All the charts and figures and plans you need to achieve a long-term dream don't have to happen overnight. For you dreamers though, you may need to take a deep breath. Patience is key. Don't get discouraged or worn down by the length of time it takes. If you will commit deeply to these goals, they will actually keep you motivated for the long haul. Some examples of long-term dreams are:

1. Start and grow your own business.
2. Be a significant supporter of women and children rescued from human trafficking.
3. Be financially secure so you can volunteer your time helping others.
4. Prepare and save so you can live comfortably in retirement without having to worry about money.
5. Fund someone else's adoption.

As you consider long-term dreams, it's important to remember that life can change *a lot* in just five years. I'm going to guess you had a dream five or six years ago that didn't happen, and you're glad it didn't. So expect your dreams to change over time—and remember, you get to determine many of those changes!

As I'm writing this book, Winston and I are working toward a long-term dream. For years we knew we wanted to move houses when our oldest started kindergarten, and we were saving for it all along. We started looking around a while back, and a new neighborhood popped up in the exact area we were looking to move. They had a few lots available, so after a lot of conversation, Winston and I decided to build a house from scratch even though we hadn't seriously considered it before.

We had heard a ton of horror stories about couples building houses together. So we went into the process with as much perspective and preparation as possible. As I'm writing this, we're now just a few months from moving in, and it has seriously been one of the most fun things we've done as a couple. We often laugh about the fact that Winston has a thousand hobbies and I don't have any. (Well, I always say relationships are my hobby because I love hanging out with my friends over a good meal!) But building this home together has become a favorite hobby for us over the past year.

Surprisingly, as wonderful as the house itself is and as much as I look forward to this next season of life in it, the process of realizing this dream has been as energizing to us as the actual finished house. There's something incredibly powerful about working toward and achieving a dream. Since I've been following the Baby Steps my whole life, Winston and I are on Baby Step 7 and are fully committed to building this house debt-free. Because of that, we tightened up our budget, saved every penny we could, and said no to ourselves *a lot*. But all of those sacrifices and staying disciplined in our spending month after month have actually been incredibly rewarding as we've worked toward our dream.

Shared Dreams

As you consider your dreams and what's most important to you, I also want you to think about the people you love the most. Shared dreams are ones you save for that involve more than just you or giving generously to someone else. They're dreams you want to accomplish *with* your favorite people.

Like I mentioned earlier, other than building our house, Winston and I don't share a common hobby. You're not going to find me taking on his love for camping in a tent in the freezing cold! And if you're married, there's a good chance you're married to your opposite too. Extroverts often marry introverts. Spenders marry savers. Nerds marry free spirits.

I love New York City. I would move there tomorrow if I could. Winston, on the other hand, would move to a duck blind in Arkansas if he could. Those things aren't going to change. I will never love the idea of living in an isolated place, and Winston would never want to live in the concrete jungle that is Manhattan. And that's okay!

Even though our personal interests are different, we're creating a life we love together. We've learned in our decade of marriage to not only support each other's passions, but also to work together as a team. The word *team* here is important. If you and your spouse are only running in separate lanes that never intersect, you're not setting your marriage up for success. Dreaming with your spouse is one of the things you can do to bring the two of you together. And as opposites, leaning on each other's strengths will help you appreciate and respect one another more.

When Winston and I dream together, we are not timid. We have some of the best date nights imagining the future. We start the conversation big like, "In five years, if money were not a factor, what would our perfect life look like?" And we go from there. Where would we travel? How would we give outrageously? Where would our kids go to school? Where would we live? Nothing is off the table. We are like little kids creating our ideal world in our imaginations. It's so much fun! And then as we see a dream come to life, we get to celebrate together and say, "Wow! We did that as a team!"

What's wild is how much dreaming together with your spouse also improves your relationship and your money. When you and your spouse agree on a shared dream, you're also agreeing on where your life—and marriage—are going. And when you agree on where your life and marriage are going, you naturally agree where your money is going. Take that in for a moment. Agreeing on a shared dream with your spouse brings so much unity to your relationship! In fact, 94 percent of people who say they have a great marriage work together on their long-term dreams.[28]

Imagine for a minute knowing exactly where you want to go as a couple and you're on the same page with your budget each month. It's not a fighting match anymore. There are no passive-aggressive moves. When you're both pulling together in the same direction, your relationship is peaceful and you can gain an enormous amount of ground. And when you're in a tough spot financially or personally, dreaming together is a way to stay motivated and keep growing together.

If you're single, it might be taking a fun summer class with your mom or a dream vacation with your best friend. If you're a single parent, a shared dream could include dreaming up a new holiday tradition with your children. You want to think through who in your life you want to build memories with and what would be a meaningful way to spend time together. Then figure out how much that experience will cost, and start saving up. Never allow your relationship status to keep you from creating a life you love. You'll miss out on a big part of why you're alive.

Okay, now that we've gone over how you dream and the different kinds of dreams, let's keep going. There's more you need to do to create a life you love!

WHAT YOU *REALLY* WANT

There are a couple of important things to keep in mind as we talk about dreams and saving for the future. The first is we need to acknowledge that not all dreams are created equally. Have you ever thought about that? In his book *A Million Miles in a Thousand Years*, Donald Miller tells the story of a man whose dream in life was to own a Volvo. This man works his whole life for this one solitary purpose, and at the end of the story, when the music should be crescendoing and all this man's hard work valiantly realized, the now old man gets in his car and . . . *wait for it* . . . drives away in his Volvo.

And the audience goes: *Uh, who cares? What's meaningful about that? I guess he gets a courtesy clap for that?*

You guys, I can totally appreciate a nice car, but our life has to be worth more than toiling away for a luxury vehicle. A nice car may be something we'd like (and it can be part of our dream), but our dreams should be bigger than a car. Dreams are supposed to pull us out of bed in the mornings. They're supposed to inspire us and challenge us and make us better. Dreams are supposed to make a real difference in the world—both for us and for others.

So when we're talking about creating a life you love, we're talking about the pursuit of what matters. The extras (think #blessed posts on Instagram) are fun, but they're just that—extra.

The other thing you want to remember is that your dream may not be what you initially thought it was. Here's what I mean: Let's say your first thought when I asked you what your dreams were was to buy a bigger house for your family. Now, there's nothing wrong with wanting more space for your people. But sometimes, it's not actually more bedrooms that you want. What you really want is to spend more quality time with family, to gather with everyone more often for holidays, celebrations, and everyday moments—and that can be accomplished in other ways that are often less expensive.

So before you go charging off to chase your dreams, spend a little time drilling down on each one. Ask yourself why you want that particular thing. Why does it hold special meaning to you? How will this dream affect those closest to you? Questions like these help you get crystal clear about what it is you *really* want.

MAKING THE RIGHT DREAMS COME TRUE

Once you've defined your dreams, you need to prioritize them. Have you ever watched someone fill a bucket with different-sized rocks? What's interesting is if you start with putting the little rocks in first, you won't ever get the big ones to fit inside the bucket. But if you start with the big rocks, you'll get the big ones *and* the little ones to fit. The same is true with your priorities. If you start with the easier shorter-term dreams, you'll run out of money before you get to the super important ones like paying off debt and saving for retirement. That's going to hurt you in the long run. But if you start with the biggies, the little ones will squeeze in there too.

The best way to prioritize your dreams is to follow the Baby Steps. When you're paying off debt (Baby Step 2), keep your dreams close, but don't spend money on them just yet. Once your fully funded emergency fund is in place (Baby Step 3), start saving for retirement (Baby Step 4) before you start saving for your dream vacay. It can take a little longer, but you can still do both. What you don't want is to end up 65 years old without enough money to live on.

If you're a dreamer and have all those new ideas every day or you're a realist with a lot of dreams, you're going to need to make some hard choices about what to save for. This is why knowing your *why* is so critical. Filter your new ideas through your *why* and your dreams to make the best decisions for you and your family. Let's say you've got two competing dreams. One is to raise your kids in the cute New England town where you grew up and the other is to teach in an underprivileged school in a large city. You can't do both at the same time so you're going to have to make a choice. Use your other dreams to help you make the decision. If your children growing up near family is another dream you have, then you'll need to put your teaching dream on hold until your kids are grown.

Once your dreams are prioritized and you've made the decision to move your family to New England, break each one down into smaller pieces and assign a dollar amount. This is where the realist in you comes into play. (Remember, we all need a little bit of dreamer and realist in us to make our dreams work.) So think about what it will take to get there: You'll have to move, probably get a new job, and search for the perfect new home for your family.

None of that will happen without money—so you'll have to save up for it. Assign a dollar amount to each step that has to happen in order to make that dream come true:

1. Search for a new job – $500 (to buy coffee or lunch for those helping you job search and to pay for help with your resumé)
2. Find a new house in the perfect spot – $30,000 (for down payment and closing costs)
3. Move – $6,000 (for moving expenses)

Then set a realistic timeframe for how long it will take to accomplish. That's your plan, and if you'll stick to it and readjust over time as needed, you'll eventually get there.

Your dream may be smaller than a complete life-change too. Maybe you just want to have the time and money to take a pottery class or to check some destinations off your travel bucket list. It's the same idea: Make a plan on paper first, and break it down into smaller steps. Then stay focused on saving for it to make it real.

Are you excited to start dreaming? Dreaming and saving will make all the difference in creating a life you love. And pinpointing your strength as either a realist or a dreamer will help you accelerate your dreams. When you're tuned in to your dreams—zeroing in on the best ones that reflect your values and your *why*—you'll be fired up to keep saving up. And the more you save, the more freedom you'll have to follow your dreams. So have those dream meetings. Make a dream board. Write a letter to your future self about what your life will look like in ten years. Dig into the *why* behind those dreams. Do whatever it takes to discover and refine your dreams. They'll motivate you when you're tired, help you stay focused on saving when life distracts you, and serve as a constant guide to you on your journey.

NOW IT'S YOUR TURN

1. Are you wired as a dreamer or a realist? How do you know?

2. Write down the big dreams you have. Be sure to include at least one short-term dream, one long-term dream, and one shared dream. (You can have more!) When you're eighty years old, what will you regret *not* doing? Be sure to spend some time drilling down what's most important about each one.

3. Now that you have your dreams written down, which ones require you to make a plan and save money? Write down the steps to get there and start saving! You can do this!

CHAPTER 12

What Motivates You to Give Money

As we've talked about your personal money mindset and why you spend and save money the way you do, I hope you've begun to see that money isn't just a math problem you need to solve. How you use money teaches you a lot about yourself. And probably the most important thing it teaches you is what's in your heart.

A friend told me about a successful businessman he knows who sold his business for $30 million. This guy was smart. He was already completely debt-free and had done some intense estate planning before he sold the company. He took most of that $30 million straight to the bank. Now if this were most of us, we'd probably buy a boat and sail away into retirement! But did he? No. He went right back into the workforce and got another job.

My friend assumed he went back to work because he liked the challenge or wanted to keep his mind sharp. But when my friend asked the guy why, the man replied: "I grew up sleeping on a literal dirt floor. I know if I go to work and keep earning money, I'll never go back to that life. I just don't want to lose my house." Even with millions of dollars to his name and two paid-for houses, this man could not shake the fear that he would end up sleeping on a dirt floor again. This guy clearly had a scarcity mindset (we talked about that in chapter 4), and the money classroom he grew up in taught him that money would make him safe. Is this a money issue? Nope. He had more than enough money. This is a heart issue—a heart issue that can hold any of us hostage for our entire lives.

It's not uncommon when I'm teaching money principles for people to look a little confused when I start talking about giving. Paying off debt, budgeting, and building wealth all make sense—until I tell them to give away a big chunk of it. Then I get a head tilt. I mean, what's the point, right? Why on earth would you work so hard to accumulate wealth if you're just going to turn around and give some of it away?

Well, that's the funny thing: Money is about a lot more than just money. I've found that most people believe if they can just get to a certain point—like having a specific dollar amount in their bank account—that they will have financial peace. But it doesn't work that way. In all my years of living and breathing personal finance, I've discovered something profound: *True financial peace doesn't happen until you're a generous, openhanded giver.* Why is that? Because giving changes you.

Here's something most people don't think about: Once you do build your net worth to $100,000 or $1 million or $100 million, if your heart hasn't been fundamentally changed by giving, your old anxiety over *not having enough* will simply be replaced by new anxiety over *losing what you now have.* Because financial peace isn't just about the math, it's possible to be very, very wealthy and still very, very fearful about money. Which is why, now that we've looked at your spending and saving, we're going to talk about your giving—and what giving gives you in return. Because it's not enough to know how to build wealth for yourself. Even if you're debt-free and have millions to your name, true peace will never be yours until you share what you have with others.

OPENHANDED OR CLOSEFISTED

There are two ways you can think about money—and both impact the condition of your heart. You can either live openhanded like you're a steward of your money and want to manage it well, or you can live closefisted like you own it all and need to keep it for yourself. Let me explain.

The Giving Scale

Imagine clutching a wadded up hundred-dollar bill in your fist so tightly no one can pry it loose from your grip—that's *closefisted,* and it's how most of the world holds their money. Many people live life looking out only for themselves. They keep everything they have—their money, time, stuff—for themselves. Generosity isn't something they think about. Sometimes people live like this because it's a cultural norm. Some people do it because of a money fear they have or because of what they learned about money growing up. It becomes a defense mechanism and is tied to a sense of security. Obviously, saving for an emergency fund, retirement, and your dreams is wise. What I'm talking about here is hoarding. It can be so easy to find your security—and even your identity—in building up a large bank account, but it leads to an anxious, empty life.

Our daughter Caroline is a toddler and has started the "mine" phase. In fact, overnight her two favorite phrases became "Mine!" and "No, I got it!" when we're trying to help her do something. Hello, Ms. Independent! If there's a toy or even a sippy cup, she'll randomly grab it and—even if no one is near her—she'll just say loudly, "Mine!" The first time she said it, Winston and I just looked at each other and smiled. We knew this (totally normal) part of parenting had begun, and we jumped at the chance to teach her to share. Toddlers love to hold tightly to their favorite toys—gripping them with an unreasonable amount of strength in their cute little fists. And we adults can be the same way with money and all the other things in life we hold dear, grasping so hard that we only grow more self-centered and fearful as the years pass.

Now picture a hundred-dollar bill sitting in your open hand—your palm is flat and that hundred dollars rests right in it. Anyone can come by and grab it. An unexpected gust of wind could even whisk it away. Viewing your money in this way—with an open hand—might seem like a bad thing at first, but it's not. *Openhanded* living means you understand that nothing belongs to you in the first place. You can apply this concept to your money, your possessions, your family, your job—anything in life. And when you're not the owner, it allows you to hold things *loosely*, making it easy for them to come in and out of your hands. When that happens, you get a front-row seat to watch how God not only uses the resources in your care to help others, but also how he continues to take care of your needs too. And the more you see God's faithfulness in action, the more your heart becomes trusting, grateful, and compassionate.

As a person of faith, I believe I'm managing everything for God. I don't own any of it. He gave it all to me, and he's entrusting me to handle his money for the good of others and for my family. I take that role very seriously, understanding that God is calling the shots with what I have. That means the money in my bank account isn't there just so I can satisfy my every desire. It's there for a bigger purpose.

This reminds me of my friend Nora who traveled to Zambia to work with several of the orphanages and schools in the area. During one school visit, a boy about seven years old snatched her Boston Red Sox hat right off her head, making a game of it. Nora played along with the boy, and they had a good laugh. But when she asked for her hat back before she left the school, the boy refused and ran away with the hat squarely on his head. This happened a lot with hats and other accessories, so Nora wasn't surprised. The kids always wanted a keepsake and were fascinated with American culture, especially anything with a logo. In fact, there were many times she gave small things—like sunglasses or a scarf—to the children she met. But her hat? This hat was special, bought in Boston after an amazing day at Fenway Park. She had a thousand good memories tied to it.

Nora felt ridiculous—and so selfish—even considering *not* leaving her hat with this sweet boy. How could she hold so tightly to a hat when it was bringing him so much joy? But this is a common human struggle—we want to keep what's ours. It's hard to be openhanded with our possessions and our money—so much so that even a Boston Red Sox hat can be difficult to release.

Nora ultimately *did* leave her hat with this little boy, but not without a fierce internal struggle. She made sure to take a few pictures with him before she left, and she now treasures those just as much as her hat. And when she drove away from the school, the boy ran alongside the car, wearing his new hat and beaming from ear to ear. It's a priceless story Nora will never forget—because in that moment she realized living with an open hand actually gave her something far greater than what she gave away.

WHY WOULD YOU LIVE WITH AN OPEN HAND?

In Luke 12:16–20, Jesus tells a parable about a wealthy man who had a heart issue:

> The ground of a certain rich man yielded an abundant harvest. He thought to himself, "What shall I do? I have no place to store my crops?" Then he said, "This is what I will do. I will tear down my barns and build bigger ones, and there I will store my surplus grain. And I'll say to myself, 'You have plenty of grain laid up for many years. Take life easy; eat, drink and be merry.'" But God said to him, "You fool! This very night your life will be demanded from you. Then who will get what you have prepared for yourself?"

There comes a point in your financial life—much like the businessman I told you about earlier—you're just building bigger barns. You trust what's in the barn to save you from sleeping on a dirt floor instead of trusting in God. You believe a bigger bank account will protect you from trouble instead of believing that God is ultimately the one who protects you. When this happens, no matter how much wealth you build, *it will never be enough.*

Even if you don't believe in God, you'll still find this to be true. Believing you have to shoulder all of life all by yourself only leads to a lifetime of fear. If you're closefisted and believe that everything in life depends solely on you, you're going to wind up exhausted and bitter. And no matter how much you have, *it will never be enough.*

The reason I teach people to start giving immediately, even before they save that $1,000 emergency fund we talked about in part 1, is because in order to obtain financial peace, you have to address both your math *and* your heart. True financial peace happens when money is your tool, not your master. And that can't happen if your soul is dependent on yourself or money.

Giving is the mechanism that helps you learn where true security comes from. Giving helps open your hand again, trusting that if you share what you've been given, your needs will be taken care of too. Giving ultimately frees your soul.

THE BLESSINGS OF OPENHANDED GIVING

When you get to that sick-and-tired moment and decide to take control of your money, all you want to see is progress. It may sound all well and good to "free your soul with giving," but really, the only thing your mind is focused on is saving up that $1,000 starter emergency fund and paying off all that debt. And I totally get it! When you look at the numbers, giving money away when you're trying to get it under control sounds crazy. That's why I want you to see what the act of giving can give *you*. So if you're new to the Baby Steps or not yet convinced giving is for you, hear me out—what you learn may surprise you.

Openhanded Giving Makes You More Selfless

The first gift of generosity is that it makes us better people. We live in a culture that's all about me, me, me. We're told to focus on ourselves, our happiness, how we feel, how we look. If you really think about it, isn't it crazy that we have a camera on the front of our phones to take pictures of ourselves? I want us to fight against that, because selfishness doesn't lead to peace or joy. It leads straight to emptiness.

We teach toddlers to share because it makes them better people. It helps them learn to think about others and express empathy and kindness. Giving is the adult version of a child sharing their toys. As adults, every time we give it makes us just a little less selfish. Sel*fless* people are better neighbors, better husbands and wives, better moms and dads, better friends, better leaders, and better team members. Giving molds us into the generous, loving, kind, and openhanded people we were meant to be.

Openhanded Giving Brings Joy

The second gift of giving is joy. You guys, we spend *so much money* buying things for ourselves that promise to make us (temporarily) happy, when it's actually giving money away that brings true joy. If you've ever left an anonymous cash gift for someone to find, you know how fun it is to watch their facial expression change when they see what you left. If you've ever given a gift to a child, you've experienced joy as they opened it. Even paying for the person behind you in the drive-through can be rewarding! The joy we receive back is worth more than the ten dollars we spent on someone's lunch. Giving increases the quality of life for the giver, the receiver, and even those who just witnessed it.

Christmastime at Ramsey Solutions is legendary. Every year a team gets together to plan our company Christmas celebration, and without fail, they blow past our expectations. In 2019, our company's operating board invited houseparents from a local children's home to join us for one of our team meetings in December. They were all invited up on the stage, and we honored them for the sacrificial work they do—and then surprised each one with $2,000 so they could buy Christmas gifts for their kids, plus an additional $1,000 just for the houseparents to spend on themselves. I looked around at our team watching all this happen, and let me tell you, we were all wiping away tears. Even witnessing openhanded living and generosity changes us.

Openhanded Giving Builds Your Faith

The third thing giving does is build your faith. We talk a lot here about working like it all depends on us and praying like it all depends on God. It's no small thing to give away some of what you depend on to provide for your family. But when you give anyway, God's faithfulness comes into sharp focus. Take Jean, for example. She's a stay-at-home mom whose husband is a public school teacher. As they were working the Baby Steps, their budget was really, really tight—but they chose to give anyway.

She said, "I remember we were down to our last dollar and praying that my husband wouldn't run out of gas before his next paycheck. Then a coworker asked my husband for a ride home after work. On the way to his house, he insisted on filling up the gas tank as a way of saying thank you. That provision was just one more reminder that when we put God first, he's faithful to care for our every need." Giving puts us in situations where we get to personally experience the faithfulness of God. And that increases our trust that God will take care of us.

THE BIGGEST REASON PEOPLE DON'T GIVE

We've looked at why living with an open hand is important for finding that financial peace we all want. Now let's look at one of the biggest reasons people don't give: because they don't make enough money.

When I talk about giving I always recommend that you start with 10 percent of your income. That's your base. It comes from the idea of the tithe in the Bible. (When you're on Baby Steps 1–3, this is all you're going to give. Then once you're on Baby Steps 4–7, you can give more than 10 percent.) Inevitably, when I say 10 percent, someone will always say, "But, Rachel, I don't make enough to give at all, let alone that much!"

If that's you, I hear you. This can sound impossible. I've sat down with a lot of people over the years and reviewed their budgets with them. Oftentimes, they show me how, by the end of the month, there's nothing left to give (or save, usually). And my response is always the same: Their budget is upside down.

One of the fun things about giving is that you get to start right away—even if you're on Baby Step 1, even if you're living paycheck to paycheck, even if you're in a massive amount of debt. Giving is "off the top," so it's the very first thing you do with each paycheck, not the last. It's even the first line in our EveryDollar budgeting app. Giving isn't something you do if there's anything left. Giving is what you do first. Then whatever is left is what you have for living expenses, getting out debt, and saving. The reason it's first is because it's that important to the condition of your heart. It's more important than getting out of debt a little bit quicker. It's more important than adding that much more to your retirement or achieving your dream more quickly. You can't shortcut your way to financial peace by skipping this step.

Now, please hear my heart on this: *I don't think you're a bad person if you haven't been giving.* There's zero shame here! But if you feel like there's just no money left over to give, I want you to understand that we all have choices in how we spend our money. Except for extreme circumstances, usually the real issue is that giving isn't a priority. Are you spending a ton of money each month at restaurants? Can you always find a way to buy the latest gadget or attend your favorite team's football games? If you are, that ultimately means those things are a priority for you, and giving is not. So how do you know what you value most? Just look back at how you've spent your money over the past few months, and your priorities will become crystal clear.

If you find yourself struggling to live with an open hand, please know we've all been there. My encouragement for you is to find out *why.* Why do you feel the need to hold on so tightly to what you have? Is it because of your money classroom? Is it because you find an unhealthy amount of security in money? Is it because you're trying to obtain a certain status to feel appreciated and seen? Are you fearful about something? Knowing why you struggle with giving will help you address and overcome whatever the issue is.

And know that if you're struggling, it doesn't mean something's wrong with you—it just means you need some help. Maybe you need more head knowledge so you can know how to take control of your money. Maybe you need to face your fears. Maybe you need help telling yourself no. There's no shame in admitting any of those things! What you want to avoid is doing nothing—because it will only hurt you in the long run.

THE BEST WAYS TO GIVE

Since giving is so foundational to achieving financial peace, let's spend a few minutes getting tactical about the best ways to give. When you're giving money, there are two ways to give: to an organization and to an individual or family. We'll look at each briefly.

If you're a Christian, I'm a big believer that the first 10 percent of your giving goes to your local church. Beyond that first 10 percent, though, there are a number of nonprofits making an incredible impact in the lives of people today. And every organization is unique and reaches a part of our world that needs help. I'm talking about everything from supporting families in the foster care system to helping people who spend their whole lives rescuing people out of human trafficking. I mean, these organizations are truly changing the world. No new car can replace the feeling you get seeing a picture of a room full of new, clean cribs you helped purchase for an orphanage in a developing world country.

As you're considering what organizations to give toward, ask yourself what you're most passionate about. What causes or non-profits make your heart beat a little faster? I would really challenge you to look around and find something to give to that you love. And I can't stress this enough: *Take the time to research the organizations you give to.* Make sure your money is really being used to help people and make the world a better place.

You can also give money to individuals in need. I love hearing stories of outrageous giving. My dad's last live broadcast every year is a giving show where people call in and share how they've experienced the generosity of others. This show is amazing! In 2019, there was a dentist who gave away free dental care for an entire day to people in his community who couldn't afford it. A single mom shared how someone gave her a place to live for several months while she was going through a divorce. Another caller talked about how, as a child, her parents were struggling financially one year. And that year they found $500 taped to their front door anonymously. You can truly change someone's life when you give them money during moments of real need. Just be sure you're really helping them with your gift, not enabling bad money decisions.

Another fun thing about giving is that it doesn't stop with your money either. You can also give your time, your talent, your resources, and your possessions. Giving your time can be anything from volunteering to just giving to others in your life. I will tell you, I have been the recipient of this several times in recent years. The number of friends and family who called or texted to help me when each of my kids was born was overwhelming in the best way possible. One of my friends came over and cleaned my entire house! Thank you, Amanda! I told her I didn't need that, but she insisted and I am forever grateful. Someone had done that for her when her first baby was born, and she said she wanted to pass that gift on. It meant the world to me.

I also had a friend who told me that after her grandfather passed away, his kids found out he had gone to the library for two hours every week to read books out loud, recording them as audio books. The library sent his family a letter thanking them for all the hours he invested in reading books for the benefit of others. In the letter, the librarian shared with them how their grandfather loved to read and wanted to share those books with people who couldn't read them. His family was stunned. They had no idea. Something as simple as sharing a couple of hours a week could forever change the lives of people in your community.

Then there's giving your talents. I get my hair and makeup done professionally from time to time for my job. One time, the woman doing my hair and I started talking about giving. Twice a year, she goes to the Nashville Rescue Mission and gives all the women there makeovers. That small act means so much to these women—for the first time in a long time they get to have their hair and makeup done. I thought that was one of the coolest ways I've seen someone give of their talents. Another friend is a photographer, and every Christmas season she opens up two weekends to take professional photos for families who can't afford them. Think of the things you're good at. What skills do you have that could help others? Then get creative and start helping!

You can also give of your resources and possessions. There was a church I spoke at last year, and they have an incredible ministry dedicated to single moms. They have a car ministry where they work on their cars for no charge. People even donate cars when it's time for them to buy a new one. Obviously, you have to be in a good spot financially to be able to donate a car, but what a gift for one of those moms! As you think about living with an open hand, don't limit your giving to money. Really consider all the ways you can live generously.

When Giving Goes on Autopilot

Now there's one word of caution I need to give you when it comes to giving: Be careful your giving doesn't go on autopilot emotionally. Giving away what's easy or convenient doesn't cause your heart to grow. In order for you to grow, you need to feel some discomfort by how and how much you're giving.

Remember how we talked about planned and spontaneous givers in chapter 4? Some planners like to automatically deduct their giving from their bank account each month. Winston and I do this because it simplifies our life. And a couple of years ago, we realized we had inadvertently fallen into an apathetic attitude toward giving. So we shook it up by increasing what we gave so it forced us to be uncomfortable. We also decided to give more of our time. With our work schedules and travel, our time is especially precious to us, so that was another way we could challenge ourselves to become more selfless. So whether you're just getting started giving or you've been giving a long time, be mindful of the state of your heart as you look for the best ways to give right now.

GIVING OVERCOMES FEAR

So many times giving feels unnecessary at best or downright scary at worst. It can be hard to give! But I want to challenge you on this. At its core, *giving is ultimately the antidote to fear.* If you're fearful you won't have enough or get what you need, the natural human reaction is to hoard what you already have. But that's the opposite of what you need to do. To overcome fear, you need to give *more.*

A lack of giving is like a warning light. It shows us that we've put our trust—our heart—where it doesn't belong. Whether you fear sleeping on a dirt floor, not being able to buy groceries for your kids, or being judged by your neighbors for driving a beater car, I want you to experience how generosity and living with an open hand will transform your heart and mind. You'll start to experience God's faithfulness in action. Your heart will grow bigger. You'll begin to see beyond yourself more and more. And the funny thing is, when you see beyond yourself, new possibilities emerge for you—new creativity, new streams of income, new relationships, new opportunities. When you live with open hands, there's room for these things to freely flow in and out. When you give, you free yourself from fear and unlock the limitations that are holding you back.

If you've never made giving a priority before, try it. Start looking for opportunities to be generous, even in small ways. See what it does to your heart, your life, and the lives of those around you. I bet you'll discover what I have—that giving truly is the most fun you'll ever have with money.

NOW IT'S YOUR TURN

1. After reading this chapter, where do you fall on the openhanded vs. closefisted scale? What steps do you need to take to get closer to the openhanded side?

2. Take a look at your current budget. Is giving the first line? Is giving there at all?

3. How has giving changed your life or the life of someone you know?

4. Take a minute to think of four specific ways you can give this month—even small ways—and commit to doing them. Be sure to reflect on those experiences and how they impacted you and others.

CHAPTER 13

How Committed Are You to Winning with Money?

I love being married to Winston Cruze. You guys, I know it sounds sappy—but I do. Being married to him has been one of the most fun and enriching parts of my life. It's not always rainbows and butterflies, but I wouldn't trade being his wife for anything.

We had been married five awesome years when we decided to have our first child. So picture this: It's December. I'm five months pregnant, and Winston and I are at home. Christmas music is playing in the background, and we're decorating our Christmas tree together—one of my favorite things to do. And all of a sudden, I start crying. Not some dainty, little cry but a full-on mini meltdown.

Obviously concerned, Winston asks, "Babe! What's wrong?"

Through tears, I tell him I love our life together so much, and I'd just realized this would be our last Christmas just the two of us. I was scared. Having a baby was going to change everything—how we spent our time, what we ate, when we slept, everything! What if giving up our life as we knew it wasn't worth it in the long run? *What if having kids ruined our lives?*

Poor Winston!

He sweetly listened to his very pregnant wife and reminded me that next Christmas we'd be celebrating with a sweet baby girl alongside us. We would still be together, and it would be even better because she would be with us. It was all going to be okay. Of course, when Amelia was born a few months later, she stole my heart immediately. I told Winston I honestly would have had her years earlier if I'd known how wonderful she would be! But the point is, no matter how miraculous and wonderful the reason for the change—change can be hard and uncomfortable, even when we know it's for the best. We usually like things that are familiar even when the *un*familiar would be better.

I hope by this point in the book you've had some aha moments about yourself, your money, and your relationships. I hope, like me, you see areas where you'd like to improve how you're handling your money. But before you rush off to change your life, I want you to raise your hand if you've ever tried to change something and it didn't happen. If you're raising your hand, you're in good company. Making a permanent change can be tricky. That's why the last thing you need to understand is how committed you *really* are to winning with money—and what to do about it. Because what I don't want is for you to discover a few interesting things about yourself, but your money and life remain the same.

COMMITTED OR INVOLVED

I was talking recently with my dad about behavior change, how some people are totally committed and able to make enormous sacrifices, while some are only involved, testing the water but unwilling to give up their lifestyle. And he reminded me of a parable about a chicken and a pig.

He said, "Rachel, the difference between being involved and being committed is the difference between the chicken and the pig in a bacon-and-egg breakfast: The chicken is involved, but the pig is committed!"

I got a good laugh out of that, but as we think about lasting change, his joke is a perfect picture for how our level of commitment impacts our lives. Take a minute to think about yourself. Is there anything in your life or money you want to change or improve? If there is, how committed are you to really changing? Are you committed or just involved? Once you know this, you'll begin to see how to get unstuck and start making real progress.

The Commitment Scale

The committed side of the scale is all in—*1,000* percent! No matter how many hurdles you face, no one can stop you. You jump off the high dive and cannonball into the deep end. You stick to the Baby Steps like glue because you believe in them wholeheartedly. The involved side of the scale is interested—but more as a spectator or someone conducting a temporary experiment. You're trying out parts of an idea without completely buying in. You're dipping your toe in the water. This is the "ish" side: You do the Baby Steps on an "ish" basis, meaning you're only doing it halfway.

Where you fall on this scale is important because there's a direct connection between how committed you are to change and how quickly you'll see real, permanent results in your life. The more deeply you're committed to the Baby Steps, the faster you'll win with money and have financial peace. If you're only involved, it will take you much longer to reach your goals, *and* you'll likely wander back into debt over time.

Now, unlike the other scales we've looked at in this book, not everyone is even on this one. This scale is only for people who want to take control of their money and are willing to take action. If someone finds the idea of budgeting or living without debt mildly entertaining but has no motivation to change their money situation, they're neither the chicken or the pig. They're at the next table over just looking at the breakfast menu. So let's talk about what *committed* and *involved* look like.

WHAT COMMITTED LOOKS LIKE

Commitment on this scale is a whole other level. You didn't wake up here out of the blue one day. Your belief and actions grew stronger over time and now they run deep. This kind of commitment means you're not straying from your position. You're doing the Ramsey Baby Steps—not your own version of them—and there is no stopping you. You're human, so you'll make a mistake here and there (thank you, grace!), but you recognize it for what it is and get back to the plan as quickly as you can. When you truly commit, the chances of going back into debt are zero.

I love talking to committed people. I was talking with one at a live event recently who shared a little of his story with us. He was $40,000 in debt right out of school when he didn't make $40,000 a year. Following the Baby Steps, he paid his debt off in under two years and was a millionaire within ten years. At that point he had extra income coming in every month and decided to lease a luxury car for $1,000 a month. Yep, you read that right. It wasn't long after he leased that car, that he realized he couldn't stomach it. The problem wasn't the payments. It was the principle. He just couldn't drive a car that he went into debt for. He no longer wanted it. He got out of the lease and then paid cash for a used car. Fast-forward another ten years. This guy is now a multimillionaire and drives a nine-year-old truck that he loves and plans to pass down to his daughter when she starts driving.

So what happened to this guy? He committed to the plan, and it changed him. It changed his financial world quickly, but it also changed *him* over time. The thing that once made him happy doesn't anymore. If you love cars and you have the money, it's fine to get a new car. In fact, if you have one million dollars or more, it's great to buy a brand-new car! That's not a problem. But what's funny is that as you're committed over time to managing your money well, your commitment will change a whole lot more than your money. It will change *you*.

Are you starting to see how all of this works together? As you spend money for you and not others, as you save in order to go after your dreams, and as you open your hand to share what you have, it changes you. And the more you do these things mindfully over time, the deeper the changes go. It's very possible to white-knuckle your way through Baby Step 2, digging your family out of debt with blood, sweat, and tears—and five years later wander into a car dealership and finance a new car you can't afford. Gutting it out only lasts so long. Commitment may start with forcing a change to your behavior, but it will lead you over time to face who you really are. Lasting transformation, the kind where you get out of debt and stay out of debt, comes from the inside out.

Not long ago I got to meet Angela. You might know her as "Debt Kickin' Mom" on YouTube and Instagram. She recently posted this on Instagram along with a photo of her new couch:

> Patience and contentment. Those two words are exactly the opposite of who I was four years ago. I used to be impulsive and always unsatisfied. It was a miserable way to live. I know now that it was rooted in a lot of emotional pain I carried with me from my childhood, but I was paralyzed by it and had no understanding of how to change. When I started the #debtfreejourney, the goal of saving as much money as possible so that we could pay off debt as quickly as possible forced me to be disciplined. It forced me to be accountable to the #budget and ask WHY I had voids in my life that spending money seemed to temporarily fill. . . .
>
> [But today] I'm a new person because . . . we waited almost an entire year since becoming #debtfree to FINALLY buy this dang couch! We saved the money several times, but things would come up and our priorities would change. Our ugly couches seemed so trivial this past year as we faced bigger things in life like a new job, a new car, saving for our retirement and college funds,

welcoming a new pet into our home . . . we didn't need, deserve, or feel entitled to a new couch. It would happen when it happened. . . .[29]

That's committed. And that's what commitment looks like over time: It transforms what you care about. It helps you become content, grateful, and patient. Yes, you spend money differently, but that's only an outward sign of how you've changed on the inside.

Commitment like this doesn't just change you either. It changes the people around you, your family tree, and those you pass it on to. Committed people can be outrageously generous because they have both the money and the emotional bandwidth to give. When you're stressed day in and day out, scrambling just to keep your family afloat, it's nearly impossible to look out and see the needs of others. This isn't because you don't have a good heart; it's because you don't have the emotional capacity to take care of anyone else. But when your money is in order and there's an overflow, it's possible to commit to help. Commitment is powerful, and it changes the world.

If you're already on the committed side of this scale, don't forget to keep injecting enthusiasm into your beliefs and habits. This is one of the reasons why continuing to dream and set new goals is so important. It's also why you're careful in how you position yourself over time. The guy who leased a luxury car came to our live event because he needed a shot of comradery, to be around like-minded "weird" people. A lot of our *Financial Peace University* class leaders say they enjoy leading FPU classes because it encourages *them* too. A number of bloggers say they track their debt-free journey online because of the accountability it gives them. Even my dad says that one of the things he enjoys about his show is that he has 16 million accountability partners. Are these people committed? Oh yeah.

But no one is a robot. I have a few close girlfriends who I can share the struggles and victories Winston and I have. We all need encouragement and community to keep us going for the long haul. Committed people intentionally look for ways to fuel their fire and keep improving.

WHAT INVOLVED LOOKS LIKE

Can I tell you one of the things I hate the most? Running. It's terrible. Like, I hate it with a passion. When it comes to health and fitness, I'm the first to admit I'm fickle. I like to blame it on the fact that the last six years of my life have been pregnancies and babies. Finding the time and motivation to work out has been *tough*. But when I'm working out, I love it and I'm all in.

Christy Wright, one of our Ramsey Personalities, is one of my best friends and my workout partner. The big difference between me and Christy when it comes to exercise is that she's a runner. Ever since I met her over a decade ago, she's run races, triathlons, marathons, half marathons—all the things. She even met her husband in a running group. I mean, of course she did. So Christy has always wanted me to run with her. Several times she's asked me to run a race with her and I politely decline, usually while laughing so hard that tears are streaming down my face.

The city of Nashville hosts the Rock 'n' Roll Marathon every year. It's a big deal here. A lot of my friends and family run it, and our company usually has a huge presence there. So a few years ago,

I realized the marathon would be five days before my thirtieth birthday. I thought, *Man, how cool would it be if I ran a half marathon before I turned thirty?* Now at that point I probably couldn't have run a mile without stopping. Running 13.1 miles seemed nearly impossible. But I knew I had the physical capabilities to do it if I trained properly. I just had to find the motivation.

When I decided to run that half marathon, I went straight to the running store to buy running shoes. Can we just talk about how expensive running shoes are? I had no idea! The sales guy may or may not have also talked me into buying running socks. And a few pairs of shorts. And two shirts. And a running belt. I spent a *little* more than I was expecting, but hey, I was a runner now and I needed running gear! I also called Christy to tell her all about my new goal and how I needed her help to create a running schedule for me and to hold me accountable. She's a strong personality, so she was going to be a perfect coach for me. She sent me my running schedule the next day, and I honestly could not wait to get started.

The first week of training was exhausting, but I felt like I was accomplishing so much, even if it was just two miles. By the end of the second week, my motivation started to go downhill. And by the end of the third week, well, I hated my life. I was miserable. That third week was my first "long" run—which was six miles—at a park on a Saturday morning. I ran the first loop, a mile, and found myself starting to mentally lose it. I knew I had to run that dang loop another five times, and I was already miserable. I ran one more loop, and as I rounded out the second mile, there in the distance was a sign from heaven. It was like God parted the clouds and a beam of sunlight shone down directly on my car. When I saw my car, everything in me wanted to quit, go home, and be with my family on that Saturday morning.

At this point in the story, I really wish I could say that I mustered up the courage and perseverance to finish that run and then, weeks later, finish the half marathon just before my thirtieth birthday. But nope. That Saturday in the park I ran straight to my car, got in, and went home! I quit! You read that correctly: I quit in the middle of the run. Some of you are thinking, *Rachel, no! Successful people don't quit!* But they do! Smart, successful people quit all the time. They quit doing stupid stuff. And I decided for me, running is stupid—and I haven't regretted that decision once.

I know running is good for you, but listen, I was not committed. The amount of change I would have had to make to my body and my schedule was not worth it to me. I had zero conviction to keep up my training. But did I go to the race as a spectator to cheer other people on? Yes! I was on the sidelines waving and shouting as the runners passed by. I was 100 percent involved—just not committed. Those who committed and finished the race received an award at the end, a feeling of great accomplishment, and a medal. As a spectator, did I accomplish any of those things? Nope. And that's what being involved means: You're watching, not winning.

You and I have the option of being a spectator when it comes to things like marathons, but money isn't a spectator sport. You don't have the option of watching from the sidelines. You *have to* handle your money. Your only choice is whether to be passive or proactive about it.

When you're just *involved* in your life and money, it's like you're sleepwalking your way through. You're sort of going through the motions, but without focus or passion. Like people who say, "I'm a believer in what you teach, but we're people who budget . . . ish." Or, "We try not to be in debt, but we sort of got a car loan last month." The "ish" mentality holds you back from winning. It slows your progress and your results.

The only way to get an all-in result is to all-out commit for the long haul. So, are you watching or winning? If you're reading this and "committed" doesn't describe you, know that you're not the only one. Most anyone who is now committed to managing their money wisely was once involved—even me. Growing up, I hated budgeting. It wasn't until Winston and I got married that I really buckled down and fully committed. I always saw budgeting as limiting and restricting. But then I learned that a budget is permission to spend, that there's so much freedom in living with a plan. I learned being committed is totally worth it—not just because of the progress you make but because of the peace of mind it brings.

If you're reading this book, I hope you want to move from watching to winning, from involved to committed. But in order to do that, you're going to have to change. Let's talk about why and how that happens.

WHY CHANGE OCCURS

When there's a change you'd like to make, it's easy to do one of two things: either dive into change without much thought and fizzle out quickly, or spend so much time thinking about it that you never get started. So let's look first at *why* change occurs and then we'll look at how to make it happen.

At its simplest, change happens when we either want out of a bad situation or into a good one. In either case, a situation arises and compels us to take action. Let's look at a couple of examples.

I talk a lot about people's *sick-and-tired moment*—a moment when they realize they can't continue on as they have been. Their life isn't working, and they're just done with the fear and stress.

Remember Angela and her Instagram post about her couch? About four years ago, she realized their family was going down the wrong road. They were on Christmas vacation when Angela got a text message telling her they'd maxed out their last credit card. She was so upset that she couldn't even sleep. That's when she sat down and listed out all their debt. She was shocked to discover it was over $77,000! Angela knew then that something had to change.

The next morning, she sat her husband down for a heart-to-heart and showed him the list. Together, they decided to make a radical change. Once they embraced that change, this family of six, living on mostly one income, was able to pay down that consumer debt in under three years. Under three years! Now they're on Baby Steps 4, 5, and 6 (which you do simultaneously), saving for retirement and college while paying off their house—and they couldn't be happier. They changed their life because it wasn't sustainable. Angela's story is an incredible turnaround, but sick-and-tired moments aren't always that dramatic. I've seen people get fed up and overhaul their money just because they got annoyed paying interest on their credit cards. The situation doesn't have to be dire—just something you're sick and tired of.

I've also seen people make hard changes because they want something more for their lives. One of our team members was doing well with her budget but realized in the dreaming process that she wanted to move to a different home in a better school district for her kids. She did her research and then sat down with her husband to determine what it would take to make the move happen.

She said later she actually assumed it wouldn't be possible—but as they talked it through, she discovered it was completely within reach in ten months. It would take some work on their part: They needed to do some repairs on their current home to get it ready to sell, and they needed to tighten their budget to save additional cash—but it was completely doable. Her dream of a long-term home for her kids in good schools was the catalyst for her change.

Whether you're getting away from a bad situation or going for something new, you're compelled to take action when the pain of making a change is less than the pain of staying the same.

HOW CHANGE OCCURS

Once you've decided to make a change, there are several ingredients you need to make it really stick. If you're missing an ingredient, it's not likely to last. I talked to Dr. Cloud about change, and he said there are really three parts to change:

1. Awareness of the problem or issue
2. Staying focused on the issue when it happens in real time
3. Intentionally and repeatedly practicing something different

We've done a fair amount of growing in *awareness* in this book by looking at your personal money mindset and what you do with money and why. By now, you've probably identified some ways you want to improve your money habits or change your money mindset. *Staying focused on the issue when it happens in real time* is where you need to think about and notice what triggers the issue in everyday life. Then you have to *intentionally and repeatedly practice something different.* That means choosing new behaviors again and again, including getting help from others. I'll give you an example of what this looks like.

Millions of people have taken control of their money through the help of *Financial Peace University* (FPU). The reason it's been so successful is because it contains all three parts to lasting change. People come to the class because *they've become aware of the issue* or are in the process of wanting change. They've had their sick-and-tired moment, or they want something better for their life.

They stay focused on their money issues and gain new tools and new ways of doing things—like how to budget using EveryDollar. They make a zero-based budget every month and track their daily spending. They stop overspending. They sell the stuff they don't need. And they notice and course-correct when they make mistakes.

FPU members also intentionally and repeatedly choose to live differently. Members meet together in small groups with like-minded people in safe, shame-free environments. The people they meet in class are supportive and encouraging. They hold each other accountable and celebrate each debt that gets paid off. They keep talking about money with their spouse or accountability partner. They keep working toward and achieving quick wins, building their motivation and enthusiasm for the long haul. And as they see their finances change over time, those new behaviors become habits. It's really amazing to watch lasting change happen when all the ingredients are in place.

But that's what it looks like when it works. What happens when it's not so easy?

CHAPTER 14

Change Your Money and Your Life

We give my dad a hard time at the office because change seems really easy for him. He and my mom's sick-and-tired moment was bankruptcy, and they've never looked back from managing their money wisely. We hear "Just change!" a lot from him. But the thing is, change isn't always quick and it's often not easy.

Lasting change is going to be difficult if you don't have all the right ingredients, but it can also be hard for other reasons. Obviously your personality plays a role in how quickly or slowly you process information and make a decision to change. Also, the seriousness of your situation impacts how you change. Like if you have a heart attack and your doctor says the only way to live is to change the way you eat, it'll be pretty easy to say no to the next steak. But those aren't the only factors at play either.

Dr. Cloud told me that, "You change quickly in areas where you don't have conflict. But if it's an area of fear or conflict, it's more difficult to change." If you've been treated harshly in the past for spending money, for example, it can be harder to stop overspending because you're still carrying the baggage from past conflict. But if you grew up in a forgiving environment, you feel free to change and stick to your budget because there isn't conflict holding you hostage. That means there are areas for all of us where it's easy to change—and there are areas for all of us where it's harder to change. Being disciplined with money may be easy for Dave Ramsey, but there are other areas of his life that aren't so easy for him. Maybe it was easy for you to change your eating habits into healthier ones, but you haven't been successful changing your money habits. Or maybe you're sold out to your daily workouts but struggle with giving generously. Know that this is normal—but it doesn't let you off the hook.

EXPECT RESISTANCE

Have you ever been fired up to change something in your life only to end up surprised when it got challenging? When you're considering a change—even if it's an easy one for you to make—you need to expect and plan for resistance. Let's look at three kinds of resistance you're likely to face no matter what it is you're changing.

Pushing Through Discomfort

Ramsey Solutions has grown so much over the years. We got to the point where we had offices in five different buildings just south of Nashville. So we started dreaming about getting under one roof and made the decision to build a new campus. The process took four years from the time the land was purchased to move-in date. Thousands of hours and details went into this new building: tons of permits, a design team and architects, contractors, and getting new utilities to the site.

The new office is a brand-new, state-of-the-art 220,000-square-foot space. And a couple of months after we moved into the new building, we broke ground on phase two of the project—adding a 200,000-square-foot tower. And every inch of this place was—and will be—paid for with cash. Winston actually spearheaded the entire project from start and finish, and I'm just so dang proud of him.

As a team we were *so* excited about all working together in this new building. It was also a huge upgrade. I mean, there is even a complete café with a full-time staff making incredible food for the team—breakfast, lunch, and for special events! Everything about this place is better than before. But the funny thing is, even as nice and new and *better* as this office is, getting here required discomfort and a ton of energy.

Even though we hired movers to do all of the heavy lifting, whole teams were exhausted by the end of their move week. It wasn't because they hauled big boxes, but because everything was new: new roads to get to work, having to figure out where to park, where to enter the building, which staircase to take, where the coffee is, which type of coffee is best, when to take lunch, where all the different meeting rooms are, the best way to set up your new desk, where the Kleenex is, where to sit for staff meetings and devotionals. Most details for an entire week were brand-spanking new, and it was exhausting! Some of us are particularly fond of our routines, so all of the disruption caused discomfort.

This is how change goes. It takes more effort and more time. But how absurd would it have been for us to bail on the new building because it required more of us? If something is worth doing, it's worth the extra effort. When you're planning for change, expect it to involve discomfort and require more energy. If you're exhausted in the early stages, just realize you're breaking new ground. Stay the course. It will get easier in time.

The Naysayers Are Back

Another type of resistance to prepare for are the naysayers—the ones who say your change isn't possible. They will tell you it's not possible to live a great life without using debt. They will say how the world is stacked against you and there's no way you can win with money in our culture today. It might be your parent, a mentor, a roommate, or someone at church who says this stuff. But let me tell you something my former pastor once said: "A man with experience is not at the mercy of a man with an opinion." I really do not care what other people's opinions are about money. Lots of people say you can't do life without a credit card, but that's not true. Lots of people say a college degree without debt isn't possible, but that's not what the facts say. The facts say there really is no such thing as "good debt."

The reality is, I have lived the Baby Steps and seen them work personally. And I've also talked to thousands of people who have followed the Baby Steps and seen them work in their lives. The facts speak far louder than any opinion. And it's the facts of experience that will change your life. As you prepare for change, *do your own homework*. Know the facts. Don't rely on someone else's opinion.

On Separate Pages

The last type of resistance to prepare for is relational. We'll first look at how this affects marriages and then how it impacts those who are single.

We hear from a lot of men and women who have trouble getting on the same page with their spouses about money. Sometimes spouses are on different pages because one is doing the budget and the other has no clue what's happening financially. In fact, in a survey done by Ramsey Solutions, we found that 88 percent of women say they are primary or equal contributors to the budgeting process in their household.[30] On top of that, only 41 percent of men report that they share in the shopping for daily needs—which means this responsibility is also being handled mostly by women.[31] Bearing the burden of your family's financial health alone is *not* healthy. At best, it's lonely. At its worst, it can be dangerous if someone doesn't know how to manage money.

Well-meaning spouses can look up several years down the road and realize they're in an enormous amount of debt. Living paycheck to paycheck can be so hard emotionally that some people even start keeping their debts and financial insecurities secret. They hide the facts from the people they love—and even sometimes from themselves. But secrets can suck the life out of you and rob your relationships of trust. Getting honest about where you are financially is hard, but so freeing! Once you bring the facts into the light of day, you'll feel better and you'll be able to make a plan together. If you're shouldering the weight of your finances alone, don't. Your money and your relationship will be stronger when you work together.

Spouses can also be on different pages because one is more committed to making progress with money than the other. This can cause major frustration and tension in the relationship. One is ready to do something extreme like sell the house and move into a two-bedroom apartment with three kids to get out of debt, while the other won't even consider cutting out restaurants or cable TV. Both spouses may want the same end result, but they aren't equally motivated to get there.

If you and your spouse aren't on the same page yet with your decision to change how you handle money, you need to address this *before* you dive into making any changes. It's almost impossible to win with money if one of you is working toward a goal and the other has zero interest in it. If you're in this position, there are a few things that can help get you and your spouse on the same page.

How You Talk About It

First, watch your tone. *How* you say something is just as important as *what* you say. Sometimes the spouse who's on board with change will attempt to persuade the other spouse by bugging or nagging them. They can do it so much that "Ramsey" becomes a four-letter word in their house. Don't do this. It's not going to work.

Also, and I think this goes without saying, but I'll say it anyway: Please don't be mean. When have you ever been persuaded to real change by someone yelling at you or shaming you? Seriously, think about the last yelling match you saw on Facebook. Did those mean-spirited words change your perspective on anything? Of course not. Be kind to your spouse. Taking control of your money should pull you together, not apart. Also remember that since you're married, it's not his and her debt—it's *your* debt together. You're a team, not adversaries.

If talking about money is a hostile conversation for you, I highly recommend you see a marriage counselor. Getting on the same page with your money is incredibly important to the long-term health of your marriage. If it's difficult to do right now, chances are there are bigger issues you need to work through.

Explain Your Why

The second thing that can help you and your spouse get on the same page is to calmly explain why you want to change how you've been handling your money. There's no nagging or yelling here. It's just an honest conversation sharing your desires and concerns with your spouse. It can also help to share what you've learned about your personal money mindset, as well as any aha moments you've had about your spouse.

Your reasons for wanting to change your money habits could be a lot of things. It could be that you're flat-out scared. Maybe it's the fear that you're not prepared for an emergency and you want that security. Maybe it's for your kids. You want to teach them a better way so they don't make the same mistakes you made. Your reason might also be that you want to do things you've always dreamed about. Maybe you've dreamed of taking a family trip once a year to enjoy one another and make memories. Remember, change happens either because you want out of a bad situation or into a good one.

Map It Out Visually

Another way to help encourage your spouse to change their money habits is to map out a visual plan. If you come home one day and randomly say, "We need to sell your truck so we can get out of debt," your spouse isn't likely to jump up and down with excitement. You're probably going to get a response like "Good luck with that!" or "Why don't we sell *your* car instead?" And for heaven's sake, don't go out and sell their car without them knowing about it! Remember that all those spreadsheets and calculations exist to serve your family. Your family doesn't exist to serve the spreadsheets.

So put all those numbers on paper (neatness counts!). Figure out how long it will take to get out of debt and how much more money you'll have each month without it. Show them in black and white how the sacrifice today will be worth it in two years (or however long it takes). Then show your spouse what your future will look like if you *don't* make a change. Seeing a finite timeline and factual plan can help them see that it's both possible and necessary.

The Power of a Third Party

The last way to get you and your spouse on the same page is to bring in a third party. I often hear from couples who have become debt-free or are attacking their plan, and initially, one spouse wasn't on board. My first question back to the reluctant spouse is: "What made you get on board?" And more than half the time they say, "I started listening to the podcast." Or, "I read one of your books." Or, "I didn't want to, but I attended *Financial Peace University* and I was convinced." Often a third party who delivers the plan helps them really hear and understand it.

Your third party could be a resource from Ramsey Solutions, but it could also be a pastor, a marriage counselor, or a Ramsey Financial Coach. Money in marriage is a huge source of tension for couples. There's no shame in asking for help to navigate that conflict and any deeper issues you're facing as a couple.

If you and your spouse aren't yet on the same page, remember to be patient with one another. You can't force anyone to change. Each person has to decide to change on their own. Your spouse may need their own sick-and-tired moment before they're ready. Walk patiently beside them through this. *Your relationship with them is more important than a self-imposed debt-free deadline.*

What's interesting is that it's not unusual for a couple to decide to start the Baby Steps, and the husband is all about it and the wife is just sort of "meh." But then a few months into the plan, she watches a bunch of Debt-Free Screams on YouTube, and the next day she's so on fire she's selling half the things in their house to bring in extra money. Her motivation ends up exceeding his. Each of us has to have our own lightbulb moment. So don't be pushy. Patience isn't a sexy topic, but it's really important to the health of our relationships.

Don't Go It Alone

If you're single, you're not facing a scenario where you have to partner with someone in order to make decisions with your money. In some ways that can be freeing. But hear me say this: It's *really* helpful to run your numbers with someone you trust. You can set up a monthly time for you two to sit down and look at your actual budget. You can even ask them to check in on you and your money once or twice a month. You're *not* doing this because you're incompetent. You can totally win with money flying solo! You're doing it because an outside perspective can be extremely helpful.

Annie, one of my best friends, is single and talks about how easy it is for singles to be a little sneaky with their spending because there's no obvious accountability in their lives. She's told me it's helpful for her to talk through big purchases (like a trip) with two of her good friends. She runs the numbers by them before she makes the decision because it helps her process the decision and also holds her accountable. Sometimes you just need an outsider or two to tell you, "It's okay to spend this money! You're in a great spot financially, so do it!"

Obviously, it can be uncomfortable to share numbers with close friends, especially if you don't want them knowing how much you make. So it does take a unique relationship to do that. But what I want you to hear is that it's worth the effort to find someone you're comfortable sharing with. There's already a lot on your plate because you're the only one bringing in money, paying the rent or mortgage, buying food, and getting the car fixed. Allow someone else to share their insight and experience with you.

Other people see things we don't. They can suggest simple ways to earn more income we hadn't thought of. They can hold up a mirror when we're spending too much on clothes. They can hold us accountable (and be our biggest cheerleader!) to finish paying off our debt when we start to run out of steam. And it's also *really* fun to be able to share our victories with another person. It might be your best friend, a coworker, a *Financial Peace University* class leader, or a counselor. Just be sure they're like-minded. The person who loves the points and airline miles they get from a credit card is just not going to get why you're doing what you're doing. Choose your person wisely.

THE POWER BEHIND REAL CHANGE

As you think about changing your money, knowing you'll need to overcome very real obstacles along the way, you're going to need something powerful to keep you moving forward. Have you ever stopped to think about what fuels change? What keeps it going? The answer is probably not what you think.

What fuels change isn't logic.

It's not emotion.

It's not even willpower.

Change happens when you *believe*. You learn about the issue. Your understanding of it grows. You discover a clear path to solve the issue. You hear from other people who have already done it. And your belief that it might just actually be possible for you to change your life too begins to grow.

When you really believe something, you have one of the most powerful, compelling, driving forces on earth: *hope*. Hope isn't some wishy-washy feeling, and hope is not a wish. *Hope is believing your actions will create a positive outcome.* Hope will cause you to sacrifice today for something greater tomorrow. When you have hope, suddenly the world opens up. Hope is incredibly powerful.

Curt Richter was a professor at Johns Hopkins who made some radical discoveries about the power of hope. Now, guys, I'm going to warn you, Dr. Richter's research isn't for the faint of heart. We're about to talk about the death of rats—I know, I know—but stick with me. What he learned will change the way you think about hope.

In the 1950s, Dr. Richter and his team studied how long rats would swim if put in a container of water with no way out. The wild rats he studied, known for their fierce, aggressive behavior, "constantly on the alert for any avenue of escape," died within fifteen minutes or less of entering the container. Fifteen minutes! This is crazy given the toughness of these wild rats. The researchers concluded: "The situation of these rats scarcely seems one demanding fight or flight—it is rather one of hopelessness; . . . the rats are in a situation against which they have no defense."[32] Without hope, the rats gave up quickly.

In later studies, Dr. Richter and his team briefly conditioned the rats before putting them in the containers. Several times they immersed the rats in water for a few minutes and then pulled them right back out. "In this way the rats quickly learn that the situation is not actually hopeless; thereafter they again become aggressive, try to escape, and show no signs of giving up." Because the rats had been rescued before, they believed they would be rescued each time they were dunked in the water. They had hope. And that hope propelled the rats to swim for *sixty straight hours—240 times longer than the rats that hadn't been conditioned.*[33] Hope was their fuel.

You know what we've discovered at Ramsey Solutions after almost three decades? The same is true for us. Everyone needs a reason to keep swimming! Hope is the fuel behind any change. When we have hope—when we truly believe we can make our life better—we're willing (and often excited) to make the sacrifices it takes. We tell people all the time to sell everything they can in order to get out of debt—even their car if they can successfully navigate the challenges of being a one-car or no-car family. This would be crazy to do just for the heck of it! I would personally question your sanity if you took that advice just because someone told you to. But when you believe you can sacrifice your lifestyle to change your life, selling your car becomes a decision you're excited to make because it's creating a better outcome for you. You've freed up money to pay off debt and save for your future; you're able to live and give like no one else; you finally have that peace of mind. Those outcomes all start with and are sustained by hope.

Evidence Builds Hope

Don't you just love weddings? The beautiful gown, the hand-picked decorations and yummy cake, the excitement and joy you feel in the room. The bride and groom stand in front of their family and friends to say their vows. And when they make their vows to one another, they say, "Till death do us part." A commitment to last for the rest of their lives, no matter what.

When you take a step back and think about it, it can honestly seem a little crazy. When a couple gets married, they don't know what the future will hold. There will be amazing times for sure, but there may also be job loss, illness, and the death of loved ones. One person might be unfaithful or even bail on the relationship altogether. So why does someone get married and risk such enormous heartache?

You only enter into something that permanent because you believe it will make your life better. *You've seen enough evidence to persuade you that it can be done—even when it's hard.* Evidence builds hope. Think about it:

1. A couple has weathered some hard stuff together while they were dating and it brought them closer.
2. They've seen each other act with integrity when no one would have noticed if they didn't.
3. They know how to fight fair.
4. They did premarital counseling together and have new tools to navigate issues when they come up.
5. They've even committed to continue going to counseling after the wedding to keep their relationship healthy.
6. They've seen other people in their life do marriage well. They know it can be done and how amazing it can be.

Couples who get married have seen enough and experienced enough to believe a strong, healthy marriage is not only possible, but also probable.

In a courtroom, what persuades a jury to commit to a decision is evidence. In the same way, different types of evidence will persuade you to believe—to spark hope within you that you can improve your money and your life. To move from involved to committed, to stay on this journey for the long haul, to overcome resistance and fear and poor money habits—*you're going to need evidence and the hope it provides.*

We all need new information in order to build a better future. If you're ready to ignite your hope, we have a ton of resources available to help you. Depending on where you are in your journey, here's where I recommend you start:

If this is your very first time connecting with Ramsey Solutions, check out *The Rachel Cruze Show* at rachelcruze .com. You can also check out my dad's show at daveramsey .com.

If you need some inspiration from real people making real progress with their finances, search "Debt-Free Scream" on YouTube.

If you want a customized financial plan, go to daveramsey .com/start. This is a free three-minute online assessment that will pull together your specific situation and get you started on a plan that's right for you.

If you need help budgeting—this is the thing that helps you accomplish all those Baby Steps!—download our free EveryDollar app.

If you're ready to dig in and get to work taking control of your finances, check out Ramsey+ at ramseyplus .com. It's everything you need to get started on—and then stay on—your journey. Ramsey+ includes *Financial Peace University*, EveryDollar Plus, and the Baby Steps tracker as well as free livestream events, a growing library of virtual courses, and an online community that will cheer you on each step of the way. If you're serious about winning with money, there's no better place to start.

If you want a different result, you're going to have to do something differently. These resources will give you a deeper understanding of what to change and how to change so you can build a life you love. Real, lasting change isn't possible until you fully commit. If you recognize that you're only involved right now, invest in yourself, your relationships, and your future by seeing and hearing the evidence for yourself.

NOW IT'S YOUR TURN

1. In what area of life has change been easy for you? What did that feel like? What area of life is more difficult for you?
2. Think about what in your life you want to change. Why do you want to make a change?
3. For each area you want to change, consider where you are on the scale of involved or committed (or if you're even on the scale).
4. What do you need to stop doing right now to better manage your money? What do you need to start doing right now?

It's Go Time

Congratulations! You made it. Everything you've read so far has been to get us to this point. My hope is you've learned a lot about yourself and how your past, present, and future impact how you handle your money today. We've talked about your childhood money classroom, your unique money tendencies, your money fears, and how you respond to money mistakes. We've also explored what impacts your spending, saving, and giving, how to make lasting changes to your money—and how all of those things affect your relationships. Now, here's where it all gets real and helps you win with money *faster*!

Take a few moments and go back through your answers to the "Now It's Your Turn" questions at the end of each section. Review what you've learned about yourself. Then create a snapshot of why you handle money the way you do by answering the questions on the following pages.

1. I grew up in the _____ Classroom.

   The challenges I face today from this money classroom are:

   The areas where I need to improve are:

2. My money tendencies are (draw a dot on each line to mark where you fall):

Saver —————————— Spender
Nerd —————————— Free Spirit
Experiences ——————— Things
Quality ——————————— Quantity
Safety ——————————— Status
Abundance ———————— Scarcity
Planned Giving ———————— Spontaneous Giving

These are the tendencies where I'm moderate and strong:

These are the tendencies where I'm currently more extreme and need to make some adjustments:

3. The major money fears I'm facing right now are:

These fears impact my money choices by:

The corresponding truths to these fears are:

4. When money mistakes happen, I respond with too much grace or not enough grace (circle one).

| TOO MUCH GRACE | ← → | NOT ENOUGH GRACE |

In order to respond with a better balance of grace and truth, I need to do this differently:

5. When it comes to spending, I typically buy things for myself / for other people (circle one).

| LOVING YOUR LIFE | ← → | IMPRESSING OTHERS |

My favorite question(s) that helps me recognize when I'm buying for others is:

These are the budget categories where I need to pay close attention to buy only what's in the best interest of me and my family:

6. I understand how saving and dreaming are connected, and know I'm naturally wired as a dreamer / realist (circle one).

The dreams I most want to accomplish in life are:

I am actively working on the following steps toward my dreams:

7. Which of the two statements below most closely reflects your view of money:

- I hold my money with a closed fist, believing it's mine to do with what I please and that my survival and success is totally dependent on me.

• I hold my money with an open hand, believing I'm to manage it well and that God will provide for me.

My favorite ways to give generously of my time, talent, and treasure right now are:

8. If I'm honest with myself, I'm involved with / committed to winning with money (circle one).

COMMITTED ⟷ INVOLVED

I know this because:

In order to increase my commitment, I will do the following every week/month:

Take all this in for a minute. This is your money snapshot as of today. Notice where you're moderate and where you're extreme. Notice where you have good habits and where you don't. Notice where you're strong and where you need help. These markers show you where you are so you can build on your strengths and make intentional changes in order to live in the Secure Classroom and truly achieve financial peace. They're also going to help you be able to talk about money with the people closest to you.

In the spending and saving chapters, we talked about the importance of your deeper *why*: your unique values and purpose that, when you let them, can drive your decisions and keep you and your money on track for the long haul. In addition to understanding your money snapshot, if you haven't already, I also want you to create your own *why* statement to help you get crystal clear about what's most important to you so you can stay focused on where you want to go and communicate that with those closest to you.

Here's an example of a *why* statement:

Money is a tool to help me do what's most important to me. What's most important to me right now is being able to change careers and pursue my passion for nursing.

The fastest way to achieve my goal is to do one thing at a time with my money. So right now, I'm focusing on paying cash for nursing school so I can graduate debt-free.

When I achieve this goal, I will take a weekend trip somewhere fun to celebrate!

My accountability partner is my spouse and I will check in with him/her about my finances at our budget meetings at the beginning of each month as well as checking EveryDollar daily to stay within budget in each category.

Now it's your turn! Fill in the blanks to create your own *why* statement.

MY *WHY* STATEMENT

Money is a tool to help me do what's most important to me. What's most important to me right now is _____

_____

_____

The fastest way to achieve my goal is to do one thing at a time with my money. So right now, I'm focusing on _____

_____

_____

When I achieve this goal, I will _____

_____

_____

My accountability partner is _____ *and I will check in with* _____ *about my finances* _____

_____

_____

MONTHLY RHYTHM

Now that you have your money snapshot and *why* statement, I want you to incorporate them into your monthly budgeting. You knew I wasn't going to let you off the hook without talking about budgeting! (I stayed away from getting too tactical too often in previous chapters, but now I can't help myself!) If budgeting sounds like a foreign concept to you, let me tell you, it is *the key* to taking control of your money.

So first thing, if you're not already, you're going to want to start doing a zero-based budget every month—before the month begins. The point of a zero-based budget is to make your income minus all your expenses equal zero.

INCOME - EXPENSES = ZERO

So if you cover all your expenses during the month and have $500 left over, you aren't done with the budget yet. You must tell that $500 where to go. And listen—the first month you do a budget, you're going to be off because you're learning! The second month will get a little better. But by the third month, your budget will start to work.

And because every month is different, you'll want to do a new budget each month. Part of doing your monthly budget is remembering that you don't actually spend every dollar! It's taking your income and being intentional with it so you can do what's most important to you. If you need more information about budgeting, we've got a ton of free teaching on this. I recommend you start here to learn more: everydollar.com/blog/zero-based-budgeting.

For your monthly budget to really be effective, there are a few things you want to do.

1. Set up a monthly time to do the budget and go over it with someone. If you're married, it's your spouse. If you're single, it's a trusted friend who also believes in the Baby Steps.
2. At your budget meeting, first review your money snapshot and *why* statement. Keeping these in front

of you each month will help you stay focused on your goals and disciplined in your spending. Be sure to update them as you change and grow over time and as your life and goals change.

3. Now look back over your purchases from last month and ask yourself the following questions:

- Was giving a priority for me? Did I experience any of the blessings of giving?
- Did I spend (or not spend) money out of fear last month?
- Did I make any purchases based on what other people would think?
- Did I stay within my budget? If not, where did I overspend and why?

4. Then look at your budget for the upcoming month and ask yourself:

- How am I going to give this month? Remember, you can give away money, time, and talents.
- Are there any places in my budget where I'm making decisions out of fear? What are the opposite truths I need to let sink in? Who can I reach out to for help?
- Are there any upcoming purchases where I'll be tempted to make spending decisions for others instead of myself? What can I do to guard against that? Do I need to change any of my social media habits to help me with this?

- Is my budget this month helping me reach my dreams and goals, or is it slowing me down? If it's slowing you down, evaluate your spending. Could you cut down spending in certain categories, like restaurants and entertainment? Spend some time thinking about your needs as opposed to your wants and go from there.
- Is there anything I need to do differently this coming month? This could include budgeting, but could also include adjustments to communication, beliefs, or boundaries.

While it may feel a little strange at first, doing this and asking these questions each month gives you a natural rhythm to check in with yourself (and your spouse, if you're married) to determine if your money and your life are on track. When you're asking these questions on a regular basis, it's so much easier to see if you missed a step or aren't making progress. And it's a lot easier to make small adjustments often in order to stay on track. Want to win with money faster? Then each month, look at where you're succeeding, where you need to make changes, and slowly and steadily keep going in the direction of your dreams and goals.

HEALTH IS MOVEMENT

I got the chance to talk with bestselling author Marcus Buckingham a while back, and he said, "We think health is balance, but it's not. Health is movement." We're built for movement, for forward motion, for progress, for growth. If you feel stuck in your money or your life, that feeling isn't there to make you feel bad about yourself—it's there as a gracious wake-up call! It's there to compel you to take action. So let's do!

I said at the beginning of *Know Yourself, Know Your Money* that I didn't write this book just to offer you some interesting moments of self-discovery that will fade with time. All of this self-awareness is to help wake you up—to realize your life and your story are not by accident. You have gifts and strengths that will take you far in life. And if you'll use what you've learned in this book to improve your money habits, you will not only win with money faster, but you *will* create a life you love.

This book also probably revealed some of your weaknesses —and that's great news! The blind spots in our lives are what keep us from living fully as God intended. So be aware of those weaknesses and faithfully address them. Doing so will get you unstuck and give you the progress and growth that marks true health.

As we close out, I want you to remember this: Money is only a tool for your life. There's nothing almighty about the dollar. Money isn't your master, and being rich has never been the goal. The goal is to use money as a tool to help you and your family live life on your terms in a way that serves the world around you. And learning to do all that begins with knowing yourself and knowing your money.

NOTES

1. Ramsey Solutions, "Money, Marriage, and Communication," The State of Money in the American Household, February 7, 2017, https://www.daveramsey.com/research/money-marriage-communication.
2. Dave Ramsey, *Dave Ramsey's Complete Guide to Money* (Franklin, Tennessee: Ramsey Press, 2012), 78.
3. Direct phone conversation with author, 2019.
4. Chapman University, "America's Top Fears 2018," Chapman University Survey of American Fears, October 16, 2018, https://blogs.chapman.edu /wilkinson/2018/10/16/americas-top-fears-2018/.
5. CareerBuilder, "Living Paycheck to Paycheck Is a Way of Life for Majority of US Workers, According to New CareerBuilder Survey," August 24, 2017, http://press.careerbuilder.com/2017-08-24-Living-Paycheck-to-Paycheck -is-a-Way-of-Life-for-Majority-of-U-S-Workers-According-to-New -CareerBuilder-Survey.
6. Board of Governors of the Federal Reserve System, "Report on the Economic Well-Being of US Households in 2018," May 2019, https: //www.federalreserve.gov/publications/files/2018-report-economic-well -being-us-households-201905.pdf.
7. Ramsey Solutions, "Money, Marriage, and Communication," The State of Money in the American Household, February 7, 2017, https: //www.daveramsey.com/research/money-marriage-communication.

8. Anna Prior, "Route to an $8 Million Portfolio Started With Frugal Living," *The Wall Street Journal*, March 19, 2015, https://www.wsj.com/articles/route-to-an-8-million-portfolio-started-with-frugal-living-1426780320.

9. Chris Hogan, *The National Study of Millionaires* (Franklin, Tennessee: Ramsey Press, 2020).

10. Chris Hogan, *The National Study of Millionaires* (Franklin, Tennessee: Ramsey Press, 2020), 21.

11. Dave Ramsey, "$700,000 in Debt and Ready to Declare Bankruptcy!" *The Dave Ramsey Show*, April 20, 2018, YouTube video, https://www.youtube.com/watch?v=CddhYTP8Kpk.

12. Brené Brown, "shame v. guilt," January 14, 2013, https://brenebrown.com/blog/2013/01/14/shame-v-guilt/.

13. Brittany Hodak, "How Bobby Bones Became the Most Powerful Man in Country Music," *Forbes*, January 6, 2017, https://www.forbes.com/sites/brittanyhodak/2017/01/06/how-bobby-bones-became-the-most-powerful-man-in-country-music/.

14. *Merriam-Webster*, s.v. "enabler (n.)," accessed 2019, https://www.merriam-webster.com/dictionary/enabler.

15. Sissy Goff, "AMKOT—Girls and Resourcefulness Part One," *Raising Boys & Girls* (blog), September 28, 2017, https://www.raisingboysandgirls.com/raisingboysandgirls-blog/amkot-girls-and-resourcefulness-part-one.

16. Wealthsimple, "Debt: A Love Story," *Wealthsimple Magazine*, November 5, 2018, https://www.wealthsimple.com/en-us/magazine/couple-debt.

17. Dave Ramsey, "Dr. Cloud Talks About Setting Boundaries (Part 1)" *The Dave Ramsey Show*, January 21, 2014, Youtube video, https://www.youtube.com/watch?v=IiZ4PQvma-s.

18. Henri J. M. Nouwen, The Return of the Prodigal Son: A Story of Homecoming (New York, New York: Doubleday & Co., Inc., 1992), 42.

19. Ramsey Solutions, Survey on Consumer Debt, 2020.

20. Maggie Parker, "Honeymoon Hashtag Hell," *The New York Times*, June 19, 2019, https://www.nytimes.com/2019/06/19/fashion/weddings/honeymoon-hashtag-hell.html.

21. Maggie Parker, "Honeymoon Hashtag Hell," *The New York Times*, June 19, 2019, https://www.nytimes.com/2019/06/19/fashion/weddings/honeymoon-hashtag-hell.html.

22. Heather Craig, "The Research on Gratitude and Its Link with Love and Happiness," PositivePsychology.com, March 18, 2020, https://positivepsychology.com/gratitude-research/#:~:text=During%20the%2021%2D day%20study,sleep%20and%20better%20quality%20sleep.

23. Oswald Chambers, *My Utmost for His Highest: Classic Edition* (Grand Rapids, Michigan: Our Daily Bread Publishing; 2017).

24. Jacqueline Curtis, "7 Psychological Triggers That Cause Spending—How to Deal With Them," Money Crashers, https://www.moneycrashers.com /psychological-triggers-cause-spending/.

25. Ramsey Solutions, "The State of Debt Among Americans," The State of Debt Among Americans Study, October 25, 2018, https://www.dave ramsey.com/research/state-of-debt-among-americans.

26. John Ortberg, *Soul Keeping: Caring for the Most Important Part of You* (Grand Rapids, Michigan: Zondervan, 2014).

27. Steven Pressfield, *The War of Art: Break Through the Blocks and Win Your Inner Creative Battles* (New York, New York: Black Irish Entertainment, LLC., 2002).

28. Ramsey Solutions, "Money, Marriage, and Communication," The State of Money in the American Household, February 7, 2017, https: //www.daveramsey.com/research/money-marriage-communication.

29. Angela Harmon (@DebtKickinMom), Instagram post (used with permission), October 26, 2019, https://www.instagram.com/p/B4FrD35 jtqcGuU6pL9GOtTwM546c85S1vuC0Zk0.

30. Ramsey Solutions, Survey on Consumer Debt, 2020.

31. Nielson, "Women: Primed and Ready for Progress," *Insights* (blog), October 14, 2019, https://www.nielsen.com/us/en/insights/article/2019/women -primed-and-ready-for-progress/.

32. Joseph T. Hallinan, "The Remarkable Power of Hope," *Psychology Today*, May 7, 2014, https://www.psychologytoday.com/us/blog/kidding-ourselves /201405/the-remarkable-power-hope.

33. Joseph T. Hallinan, "The Remarkable Power of Hope," *Psychology Today*, May 7, 2014, https://www.psychologytoday.com/us/blog/kidding-ourselves /201405/the-remarkable-power-hope.

KNOW YOURSELF, KNOW YOUR MONEY
Endorsements

Rachel does such a great job of getting to the root of why we make the money decisions (and mistakes) we do. This book is a self-discovery necessity.

—*Marcus Buckingham, researcher,* New York Times *bestselling author, and founder of the Strengths Revolution*

I have often said if you want to understand someone, look at their checkbook and their calendar. How we spend time and money says a lot about who we are. Rachel goes deep into unraveling that mystery.

—*Dr. Henry Cloud,* New York Times *bestselling author*

We are all eventually faced with the responsibility of managing finances! It is an important and inevitable part of life. Rachel Cruze dives deep into why we interact with money the way we do. She teaches the importance of understanding yourself in order to make real progress toward your money goals!

—*Candace Cameron Bure, actress and* New York Times *bestselling author*

If you want to be better at something, put better people around you. That's what this book is! It's a better person around you that's also looking out for you. I grew up very poor, so I had no money and no one to teach me about money. This book was perfect for me then. And frankly, it's perfect for me now. Start reading. Get smarter. Make better decisions. Live better. The end!

—*Bobby Bones, #1* New York Times *bestselling author and national radio personality*

When you understand the *why* behind your money decisions, you can make real progress toward your goals. This book will not only change your money habits, it'll also improve your relationships—and your life!

—Christine Caine, founder of A21 and Propel Women

Rachel Cruze understands how to simplify complex ideas. *Know Yourself, Know Your Money* unravels the motives and mindset behind the unfortunate financial and lifestyle decisions people make, and then provides a clear plan for lasting change. This book is must-read for anyone who struggles with money and personal identity.

—The Minimalists Joshua Fields Millburn and Ryan Nicodemus, authors, podcasters, filmmakers, and public speakers

If you're ready to think deeply about why you spend money the way you do and get practical help in moving forward, this book is for you! You will love it!

—Jennie Allen, New York Times *bestselling author of* Get Out of Your Head *and founder and visionary of* IF:Gathering

This may be the most helpful book on personal finance you ever read! Rachel will help you understand yourself and your money in ways you never imagined.

—Annie F. Downs, bestselling author of 100 Days to Brave *and host of* That Sounds Fun *podcast*

This book is a GAME-CHANGER for anyone looking to create and live a life they love! Rachel puts us on a path of self-discovery to understand why we handle money the way we do and how that knowledge can deepen our relationships with others.

—Paula Faris, journalist, author, and podcaster

This book gives you a clear view of why you relate to money the way you do, plus a practical path toward changing your money habits for the better. You have to read it!

—Drs. Les & Leslie Parrott, #1 New York Times *bestselling authors* of Saving Your Marriage Before It Starts

The title says it all! Understanding who you are and how you're wired is a crucial first step to revolutionizing your financial habits. Practical and accessible, this book will take you on a journey of self-discovery that will open your eyes to how your past affects the way you view money in the present, and how your dreams for the future impact your financial life. It's a life-changer that I can't recommend highly enough!

—Ian Morgan Cron, *bestselling author of* The Road Back to You

Know Yourself, Know Your Money shines light on motives and money. It expertly leads the reader to see and benefit from knowing their emotional motivation related to money. It is a great book—witty, profound, practical, and spiritual, all wrapped up as a well-written gift for the reader.

—Chip Dodd, *PhD and bestselling author of* The Voice of the Heart

BUILD *Better* MONEY HABITS

RAMSEY+

A Money Plan for Real Life

You've just unlocked *why* you handle money the way you do. Now, it's time to put that *why* to work.

With Ramsey+, you'll save an emergency fund, pay off your debt, create monthly budgets that work, invest for your future, and make progress toward the goals that matter most to you. Build better money habits and create the future you want! Ramsey+ will be with you every step of the way.

P.S. In Ramsey+, you'll find a video course from Rachel that brings this book to life!

Start Your Free Trial

Visit ramseyplus.com/knowyourmoney.

Build a Life You'll Love
with Rachel's #1 Bestseller

Now that you understand why you handle money the way you do, it's time to dive into the seven powerful money habits that will help you live the life of your dreams—without debt, stress, and worry! *Love Your Life, Not Theirs* will empower you to quiet the comparisons, avoid debt, save for the future, and communicate in a healthy way about money.

Get your copy today at **rachelcruze.com/store**.